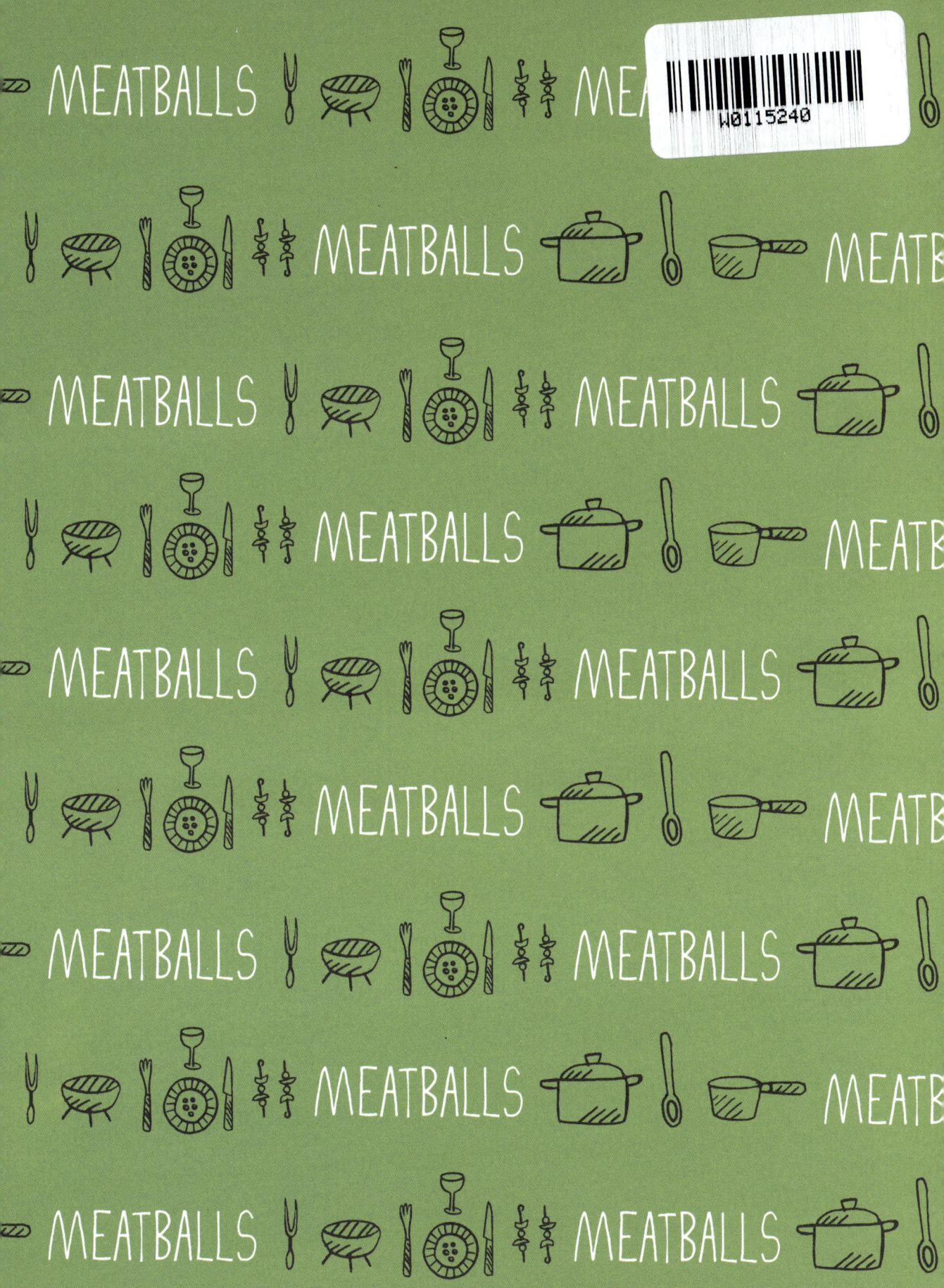

Recipes and styling by Valéry Drouet
Photos by Pierre-Louis Viel

VALÉRY DROUET & PIERRE-LOUIS VIEL

MEATBALLS

[FALAFELS, SKEWERS, AND MORE]

h.f.ullmann

CONTENTS

SAUCES

MARINADES

MEATBALLS

Meatballs

Fishballs

SKEWERS

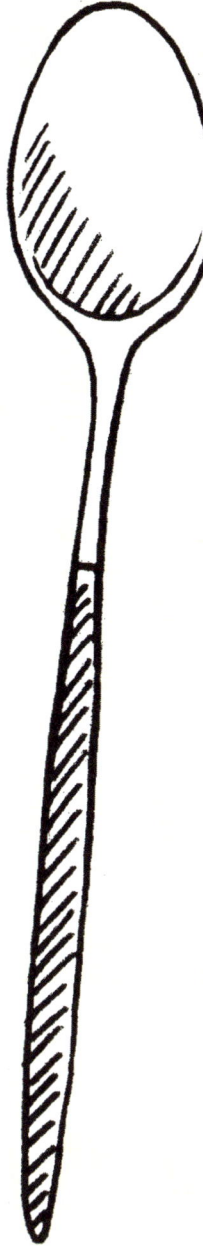

SAUCES

ORIENTAL SAUCE

CARAMELIZED SHALLOTS

SWEET AND SOUR SAUCE

WHITE SAUCE WITH MINT

HOT CHILI SAUCE

PINEAPPLE CHUTNEY

SAUCES

ORIENTAL SAUCE

Serves 6/Preparation: 15 minutes/No cooking

Peel and chop 1 small yellow onion and 2 garlic cloves. Wash and chop 2 sprigs cilantro. In a bowl, mix 1 tablespoon harissa with 1 tablespoon lukewarm water. Add a generous ¾ cup (200 g) homemade mayonnaise, the onion, garlic, and cilantro and mix together. Keep the sauce in the refrigerator.

Ideal with meatballs and skewers of lamb or chicken.

CARAMELIZED SHALLOTS

Serves 6/Preparation: 20 minutes/Cooking time: 30 minutes

Peel a generous 1 lb (500 g) shallots and slice thinly lengthways. Cook in a sauteuse pan with 2½ tablespoons (40 g) butter for 5 minutes over low heat. Add 4½ tablespoons (60 g) granulated sugar and mix until the shallots are well covered. Add ⅔ cup (400 ml) white wine and season with salt and pepper. Bring to a boil, then cook for 25–30 minutes over medium heat until the shallots are caramelized.

Ideal with meatballs and skewers of lamb, chicken, veal or beef.

SWEET AND SOUR SAUCE

Serves 6/Preparation: 15 minutes/Cooking time: 30 minutes

Peel 1 medium yellow onion and chop finely. Place in a saucepan. Add ⅔ cup (150 ml) red wine vinegar, 5 tablespoons (70 g) granulated sugar, 7 tablespoons (100 ml) water, 2 pinches ground chili and salt. Bring to a boil, then cook for 30 minutes over medium heat, stirring regularly. Turn off the heat and allow the sauce to cool.

Ideal with skewers and balls of fish, shrimp, pork or chicken.

WHITE SAUCE WITH MINT

Serves 6/Preparation: 15 minutes/No cooking/ Refrigeration: 1 hour

Peel 1 medium yellow onion and 2 garlic cloves and chop finely. Wash and chop 20 fresh mint leaves. In a bowl, mix 1 cup (250 g) fromage blanc with salt and pepper, to taste, 2 tablespoons olive oil and the juice of 1 lemon. Add the onion, garlic, and mint and mix together. Refrigerate the sauce for 1 hour before serving.

Ideal with balls and skewers of veal, lamb or vegetables, koftas, and fish croquettes.

HOT CHILI SAUCE

Serves 6/Preparation: 20 minutes/Cooking time: 30 minutes

Seed 1 long red chili and slice thinly. Peel 3 large shallots and slice thinly. Place the chili, shallots, 2 tablespoons granulated sugar, 3 tablespoons nuoc nam, scant 1 cup (200 ml) rice vinegar, 1½ tablespoons freshly grated ginger, 3½ tablespoons (50 ml) water, and salt and pepper to taste, in a saucepan. Mix together and cook for 30 minutes over medium heat. Turn off the heat and allow the sauce to cool.

Ideal with skewers and balls of fish or pork.

PINEAPPLE CHUTNEY

Serves 6/Preparation: 20 minutes/Cooking time: 1 hour

Peel and chop 2 large shallots and 2 garlic cloves. Seed 1 small mild chili and chop. Peel 9 oz (250 g) pineapple and cut in small cubes. Place the pineapple cubes, shallots, garlic, and chili in a saucepan. Add ⅓ cup (75 g) granulated sugar, ⅔ cup (150 ml) wine vinegar, 7 tablespoons (100 ml) water, salt, and pepper. Mix together and simmer for 1 hour over low heat. Leave to cool. Keep the chutney in a pot in the refrigerator.

Ideal with balls and skewers of veal, chicken or pork.

MARINADES

ANISE MARINADE

THAI MARINADE

INDIAN MARINADE

SPICED MARINADE

CITRUS FRUIT MARINADE

GREEN MARINADE

MARINADES

ANISE MARINADE

Serves 6/Preparation: 15 minutes/Marinating: about 2 hours

In a bowl, mix 3½ tablespoons (50 ml) lemon juice with 2 tablespoons pastis, salt, and pepper. Beat in ⅔ cup (150 ml) olive oil, then mix in 2 tablespoons fennel seeds and 1 tablespoon lemon thyme leaves.

Ideal for marinating skewers of chicken, tuna, swordfish, or cod.

THAI MARINADE

Serves 6/Preparation: 20 minutes/Marinating: about 4 hours

Peel and grate 1 oz (30 g) fresh ginger. Peel and chop 3 garlic cloves. Remove the seeds from 1 small, strong red chili and slice thinly. Wash and chop 20 leaves Thai or classic basil (or cilantro). Mix all the ingredients in a bowl. Add ⅔ cup (150 ml) sweet soy sauce and 7 tablespoons (100 ml) salt soy sauce.

Ideal for marinating skewers of shrimp, fish, chicken, or duck.

INDIAN MARINADE

Serves 6/Preparation: 20 minutes/ Marinating: about 4 hours

In a bowl, mix 1 large tablespoon curry powder, salt, and pepper, to taste, with 3½ tablespoons (50 ml) hot water. The curry powder must be thoroughly dissolved. Leave to cool. Peel 1 red onion and slice thinly. Add the juice of ½ lemon to the curry, then beat in 7 tablespoons (100 ml) olive oil. Stir in the sliced onion.

Ideal for marinating skewers of beef, lamb, or pork.

SPICED MARINADE

Serves 6/Preparation: 15 minutes/Marinating: about 4 hours

Wash and chop ½ bunch of cilantro. Peel and chop ½ red onion. In a bowl, mix 1 large tablespoon harissa with 3½ tablespoons (50 ml) hot water, 2 tablespoons lemon juice, and salt. Beat in 7 tablespoons (100 ml) olive oil. Add the onion and cilantro and mix well.

Ideal for marinating skewers of lamb or beef.

CITRUS FRUIT MARINADE

Serves 6/Preparation: 15 minutes/Marinating: about 2 hours

Wash 1 lime, remove and chop the peel. Squeeze 3 large oranges, 2 limes, and 1 lemon. In a bowl, mix the citrus fruit juices with salt and pepper, and 1 good pinch chili powder. Beat in 7 tablespoons (100 ml) olive oil, then mix in the chopped lime peel.

Ideal for marinating skewers of fish or chicken.

GREEN MARINADE

Serves 6/Preparation: 15 minutes/Marinating: about 4 hours

Wash and chop ½ bunch of chervil, 3 sprigs of tarragon, and 1 small bunch of flat-leaf parsley. Peel 2 large shallots and chop finely. In a bowl, mix the juice of 1 lemon with salt and pepper. Beat in 7 tablespoons (100 ml) olive oil. Lastly, mix in all the herbs and the chopped shallots.

Ideal for marinating skewers of chicken, tuna, swordfish, or smoked haddock.

MEATBALLS

Meatballs of chicken with goat's cheese, pistachios, and figs

PREPARATION: 40 minutes
COOKING TIME: 25 minutes

INGREDIENTS

Serves 6

- 4 large chicken breasts
- generous ¾ cup (100 g) pistachios, shelled and skinned
- 1 yellow onion
- 6½ oz (180 g) ash-coated goat's cheese
- 6 ripe figs
- 3½ tbsp (50 ml) olive oil
- 2 tbsp honey
- salt, freshly ground pepper

» Grind the chicken breasts in a food processor. Grind the pistachios very finely. Peel and chop the onion.

» Cut the goat's cheese, into small pieces. Cut the figs into small cubes.

» In a saucepan, sweat the onion in 2 tablespoons of the olive oil for 5 minutes over low heat. Add the figs and honey; caramelize lightly for 2 minutes over medium heat, stirring continuously. Leave to cool.

» Pre-heat the oven to 340 °F (170 °C).

» In a large bowl, mix the ground chicken with the fig mixture, the pieces of chèvre, and a quarter of the ground pistachio.

» Tip the remaining ground pistachio onto a plate. Form balls the size of a large walnut and roll in the pistachio, pressing down lightly to make it stick.

» Arrange the balls on a baking sheet lined with parchment and drizzle with the remaining olive oil. Cook in the oven for 20—25 minutes. Serve very hot with baked tomatoes and a herb salad.

These meatballs can be served with a sweet-and-sour sauce (see recipe p. 12).

MEATBALLS OF CHICKEN WITH WOOD EAR MUSHROOMS

PREPARATION: 30 minutes
SOAKING: 10 hours
COOKING TIME: 20 minutes

INGREDIENTS

Serves 6

- generous 1 lb (500 g) chicken breast
- 1½ oz (40 g) dried wood ear mushrooms
- 1 medium yellow onion
- 1¼ oz (50 g) golden sesame seeds
- 3 tbsp nuoc nam
- 2 tbsp oyster sauce
- 3½ tbsp (50 ml) salt soy sauce
- ⅔ cup (150 ml) teriyaki sauce
- 3½ tbsp (50 ml) sunflower oil
- salt, freshly ground pepper

» The day before, soak the dried wood ear mushrooms in a large container of cold water to rehydrate them.

» On the actual day, drain the wood ear mushrooms. Cut a quarter of them into large pieces and chop the remainder finely.

» Grind the chicken breasts in a food processor.

» Peel and chop the onion. Sweat in a skillet with half the oil for 5 minutes over medium heat. Add the chopped mushrooms, nuoc nam, and oyster sauce. Mix together and leave to cool.

» In a large bowl, mix the ground chicken with the mushroom mixture, salt, and pepper. Form into walnut-sized balls.

» In a skillet, seal the meatballs rapidly over high heat in the remaining oil. Add the soy sauce and teriyaki sauce to the pan. Add the mushroom pieces and cook for 5 minutes over high heat, stirring the meatballs into the sauce so they are thoroughly coated.

» Serve very hot with flavored rice.

MEATBALLS OF CHICKEN WITH CASHEW NUTS AND CILANTRO

PREPARATION: **30 minutes**
COOKING TIME: **30 minutes**

INGREDIENTS

Serves 6

- 1¾ lb (750 g) chicken breast
- 11 oz (300 g) cashew nuts
- 3½ tbsp (50 ml) milk
- 2 slices of bread, without crusts
- 1 medium yellow onion
- 2 garlic cloves
- 1 small stick celery
- 4 sprigs cilantro
- 7 tbsp (100 ml) olive oil
- 2 tbsp liquid honey
- 1 egg
- salt, freshly ground pepper

≫ Grind the chicken breasts in a food processor.

≫ Grind the cashew nuts, but not too finely.

≫ Pour the milk into a bowl and crumble the bread into it. Leave to soak for 10 minutes.

≫ Peel and chop the onion and garlic cloves. Wash the celery and remove any strings, then cut into small cubes. Wash and chop the cilantro.

≫ In a skillet, sweat the onion, garlic, and celery for 5–6 minutes over medium heat in half the olive oil. Add half the ground cashews and the honey and cook for 4–5 minutes, stirring continuously. Turn off the heat and add the cilantro. Leave to cool.

≫ Pre-heat the oven to 355 °F (180 °C).

≫ In a large bowl, mix the ground chicken with the cashew nut mixture. Season with salt and pepper to taste. Squeeze out the breadcrumbs and add them with the egg to the bowl. Mix together by hand until smooth and even. Form into balls the size of a large walnut and roll in the remaining ground cashews.

≫ Arrange the meatballs on a baking sheet lined with parchment and drizzle lightly with the remaining olive oil. Bake in the oven for 25–30 minutes. Serve very hot with homemade fries and sweet-and-sour sauce.

MEATBALLS OF PORK WITH GROUNDNUTS AND RED ONION

PREPARATION: **30 minutes**

COOKING TIME: **25 minutes**

INGREDIENTS

Serves 6

- 1¾ lb (800 g) pork sausage meat
- 5½ oz (150 g) salted groundnuts
- 1 large red onion
- 1 small bunch cilantro
- ⅓ cup (80 ml) olive oil
- 2 large tablespoons liquid honey
- 7 tbsp (100 ml) sweet soy sauce or teriyaki sauce
- 1½ tbsp (25 g) butter
- salt, freshly ground pepper

For the sauce
- 3 tbsp homemade mayonnaise
- 1 tbsp ketchup
- a few drops Tabasco®
- salt

≫ Make the sauce: in a bowl, mix the mayonnaise with the ketchup, Tabasco®, 2 tablespoons cold water, and salt, to taste. Keep refrigerated.

≫ Chop the groundnuts. Peel and chop the onion. Wash and chop the cilantro.

≫ In a skillet, sweat the onion in half the olive oil for 6–8 minutes over medium heat. Add the groundnuts and honey, mix together and cook for a further 5 minutes over low heat. Turn off the heat and mix in the cilantro. Leave to cool.

≫ In a large bowl, mix the sausage meat with the groundnut mixture, salt, and pepper. Form into walnut-sized balls.

≫ In a skillet, brown the meatballs in the remaining oil and the butter for 8–10 minutes over medium heat, rolling them around so they brown evenly. Then add the soy or teriyaki sauce and continue rolling to coat the meatballs lightly. Serve very hot with the sauce.

> Try these meatballs in pita or naan bread with a few leaves of lettuce and thin slices of red onion.

PREPARATION: **50 minutes**
COOKING TIME: **20 minutes**

INGREDIENTS

Serves 6

- 1¾ lb (750 g) sausage meat
- 7 oz (200 g) caul fat (from your butcher)
- 2 stems lemongrass
- 2 medium yellow onions
- 3½ tbsp (50 ml) olive oil
- 3 tbsp nuoc nam
- 3 tbsp oyster sauce
- ⅔ cup (150 ml) teriyaki sauce
- salt, freshly ground pepper

MEATBALLS OF PORK WITH LEMONGRASS, WRAPPED IN CAUL FAT

≫ Soak the caul fat in a large bowl of cold water.

≫ Remove the outer leaves of the lemongrass and slice the tender part of the stem. Peel and chop the onions.

≫ In a saucepan, sweat the onions and lemongrass in half the olive oil for 8–10 minutes over medium heat. Add the nuoc-nam, oyster sauce, pepper, and a little salt. Mix together and cook for a further 3–4 minutes. Leave to cool.

≫ In a large bowl, mix the sausage meat with the onion-and-lemongrass mixture. Form into balls the size of a large walnut.

≫ Rinse the caul fat in cold water and squeeze with your hands to extract as much water as possible. Stretch it out on the worktop and cut in squares of 4–5 inches (10–12 cm).

≫ Wrap each ball in 1 square of caul fat. Thread the wrapped balls in pairs on wooden sticks (or lemongrass stems).

≫ Heat the remaining oil in a large skillet and cook the meatballs for 10–12 minutes over medium heat, turning frequently. Turn up the heat a little and add the teriyaki sauce to the pan. Cook for a further 8–10 minutes, basting the meatballs regularly with sauce using a spoon and turning them so they are well coated.

≫ Serve immediately with rice or a salad of Chinese cabbage and herbs.

Meatballs of pork with melting Camembert centers

PREPARATION: **30 minutes**

COOKING TIME:
12–15 minutes

INGREDIENTS

Serves 6

- 1¾ lb (750 g) pork sausage meat
- 2 slices crumbly bread
- 3½ tbsp (50 ml) milk
- 1 yellow onion
- 3 sprigs tarragon
- 3½ tbsp (50 ml) sunflower oil
- 7 oz (200 g) raw-milk Camembert
- 2 tbsp flour
- salt, freshly ground pepper

>> Remove the crusts from the bread. Crumble the bread into a bowl and add the milk. Set aside.

>> Peel and chop the onion. Pick the leaves off the tarragon and chop.

>> In a skillet, sweat the onion in 1 tablespoon of oil for 6–8 minutes over medium heat. Leave to cool.

>> Cut the Camembert in large cubes.

>> In a large bowl, mix the sausage meat with the onion, the squeezed-out breadcrumbs, tarragon, salt, and pepper. Form into balls the size of a large walnut. Make a hole in each ball with your thumb, insert 1 cube of Camembert, then reshape the ball.

>> Sprinkle the flour on a plate and roll the meatballs in it until thoroughly coated.

>> Heat the remaining oil in a large skillet and brown the meatballs for 12–15 minutes over medium heat, turning regularly. Serve very hot with a salad or a potato gratin.

You can add small cubes of apple to the sausage meat. Cut 1 Golden Delicious apple in cubes and sweat for 5 minutes in a skillet over medium heat with 1½ tablespoons butter and 2 tablespoons sugar.

MEATBALLS OF VEAL WITH SHIITAKE MUSHROOMS AND WASABI

PREPARATION: **30 minutes**
COOKING TIME: **15 minutes**

INGREDIENTS

Serves 6

- 1¼ lb (600 g) ground veal
- 14 oz (400 g) shiitake mushrooms
- 2 shallots
- 3½ tbsp (50 ml) sunflower oil
- 2 tbsp liquid honey
- 1 teaspoon wasabi
- 3½ tbsp (50 ml) sweet soy sauce
- salt, freshly ground pepper

≫ Carefully clean the shiitake mushrooms with a damp cloth or a small brush and chop roughly. Peel the shallots and chop finely.

≫ In a skillet, sweat the shallots in half the oil for 3 minutes over medium heat. Add the shiitake mushrooms, season with salt and pepper, and cook for 4–5 minutes over medium heat, stirring continuously. Add the honey and caramelize lightly. Turn off the heat and leave to cool.

≫ In a large bowl, mix the shiitake mushrooms mixture with the ground veal, wasabi, salt, and pepper. Form into balls the size of a small walnut.

≫ Heat the remaining oil in a skillet and cook the meatballs for 8–10 minutes over medium heat. Add the soy sauce to the pan, stir to cover the meatballs well and cook for a further 4–5 minutes over medium heat to reduce the sauce and lightly coat the meatballs.

≫ Serve very hot on a bed of crisp lettuce and, if desired, with wasabi.

MEATBALLS OF VEAL AND PIPERADE WRAPPED IN CAUL FAT

PREPARATION: **45 minutes**
COOKING TIME: **30 minutes**

INGREDIENTS

Serves 6

- 1¾ lb (800 g) ground veal (shoulder or other)
- 4 oz (200 g) caul fat (from your butcher)
- 2 red bell peppers
- 1 yellow bell pepper
- ½ onion
- 2 garlic cloves
- 10 basil leaves
- 3½ tbsp (50 ml) olive oil
- 2 sprigs thyme
- salt, freshly ground pepper

≫ Soak the caul fat in a container of cold water.

≫ Peel and seed the bell peppers, and cut in small cubes. Peel and chop the half-onion and the garlic cloves. Wash and chop the basil.

≫ In a skillet, sweat the onion and garlic in half the olive oil for 3 minutes over low heat. Add the bell peppers, the sprigs of thyme, and salt and pepper to taste. Cook for 12–15 minutes over medium heat, stirring regularly. Turn off the heat, mix in the basil. Leave to cool.

≫ In a large bowl, mix the ground veal with the cooked peppers, salt, and pepper. Form into walnut-sized balls.

≫ Drain the caul fat and squeeze with your hands to extract as much water as possible. Cut the caul fat in small squares. Wrap each meatball tightly in 1 square of caul fat.

≫ Heat the remaining oil in a skillet over medium heat and cook the meatballs for 6–8 minutes. Turn them over, reduce the heat a little and cook for a further 8–10 minutes until golden brown.

≫ Serve hot with braised carrots and a mixed salad.

Meatballs of veal stuffed with mozzarella and wrapped in Parma ham

PREPARATION: **30 minutes**
COOKING TIME: **15 minutes**

INGREDIENTS

Serves 6

- 1½ lb (700 g) ground veal
- 2 slices crumbly bread
- ⅓ cup (80 ml) milk
- 1 onion
- 7 oz (200 g) mozzarella
- 1 tbsp pistou
- 24 very thin slices Parma ham
- 1 cup (250 ml) balsamic vinegar
- 1 tbsp granulated sugar
- 1 tbsp (15 g) butter
- 3½ tbsp (50 ml) olive oil
- salt, freshly ground pepper

≫ Remove the crusts from the bread. Crumble the bread in a bowl and cover with the milk.

≫ Peel the onion and chop finely. Cut the mozzarella in 24 small cubes.

≫ In a large bowl, using your hands, mix the ground meat with the onion, pistou, squeezed breadcrumbs, and salt and pepper to taste.

≫ Form 24 balls the size of a large walnut. Push 1 cube of mozzarella into the middle of each ball and reshape the ball. Roll each ball fairly tightly in 1 slice of Parma ham and refrigerate.

≫ In a saucepan, bring the balsamic vinegar and sugar to a boil and reduce over medium heat until the vinegar becomes slightly syrupy. Beat in the butter. Keep this sauce hot (without boiling).

≫ Pre-heat the oven to 355 °F (180 °C).

≫ Heat the olive oil in a large skillet and brown the meatballs for 4–5 minutes over medium heat. Transfer to an oven dish and bake in the oven for 8–10 minutes.

≫ Serve very hot with the balsamic vinegar sauce.

MEATBALLS OF VEAL WITH PINE NUTS AND GORGONZOLA

PREPARATION: **40 minutes**
COOKING TIME: **20 minutes**

INGREDIENTS

Serves 6

- 1¾ lb (750 g) ground veal
- ⅔ cup (100 g) pine nuts
- 2 garlic cloves
- 1 medium yellow onion
- 10 basil leaves
- 9 oz (250 g) Gorgonzola
- ¾ cup (100 g) flour
- 1¼ cups (300 ml) light whipping cream
- 7 tbsp (100 ml) olive oil
- salt, freshly ground pepper

» Toast the pine nuts in a dry skillet for 3 minutes over low heat, then chop them roughly.

» Peel and chop the garlic cloves and the onion. Wash and chop the basil leaves. Cut the Gorgonzola in small pieces.

» In a large bowl, using your hands, mix the ground meat with 5½ oz (150 g) Gorgonzola, the pine nuts, garlic, onion, basil, salt, and pepper. Form into balls the size of a small walnut, roll them in the flour, and refrigerate.

» In a large saucepan, bring the cream to a boil with salt and pepper for 5 minutes over medium heat. Add the remaining Gorgonzola and boil for 5 minutes, stirring continuously. Then mix with a hand mixer to give a smooth, creamy sauce.

» Heat the olive oil in a large skillet and brown the meatballs for 8—10 minutes over medium heat. Then drop them into the pan of Gorgonzola sauce and simmer for 8—10 minutes over low heat.

» Serve with linguini or spaghetti with basil.

POLPETTE

PREPARATION: 30 minutes
COOKING TIME: 15 minutes

INGREDIENTS

Serves 6

- 2 lb (900 g) ground veal
- 3½ tbsp (50 ml) milk
- 4 slices bread, without crusts
- 5 garlic cloves
- 1 bunch flat-leaf parsley
- 15 basil leaves
- 3 oz (90 g) Parmesan
- 3 oz (90 g) pecorino
- 2 large eggs
- 1 large yellow onion
- 7 tbsp (100 ml) olive oil
- 4 cups (1 liter) tomato purée
- ⅔ cup (100 g) flour
- salt, freshly ground pepper

≫ Pour the milk into a bowl. Crumble the bread and soak in the milk.

≫ Peel and chop 3 garlic cloves. Wash and chop the parsley and 10 leaves of basil. Grate both cheeses.

≫ In a large bowl, using your hands, mix the ground meat with the chopped garlic, squeezed breadcrumbs, eggs, grated cheeses, chopped parsley and basil, and salt and pepper. Form into balls the size of a large walnut and refrigerate.

≫ Peel and chop the onion and the remaining garlic cloves.

≫ In a casserole, sweat the onion and garlic in half the olive oil for 5 minutes over medium heat. Add the tomato purée, generous ¾ cup (200 ml) of water, salt, and pepper. Cook for 10 minutes over medium heat.

≫ Meanwhile, roll the meatballs in the flour, then brown rapidly in a large skillet over high heat in the remaining olive oil. Transfer to the casserole, cover and cook for 45 minutes over low heat.

≫ Chop the remaining basil and sprinkle over the polpette.

≫ Serve very hot, with fresh pasta and grated Parmesan.

MEATBALLS OF BEEF WITH PAPRIKA

PREPARATION: **30 minutes**
COOKING TIME: **50 minutes**

INGREDIENTS

Serves 6

- 1¾ lb (800 g) ground beef
- 4 oz (120 g) linseed
- 3 yellow onions
- ½ tbsp (50 ml) sunflower oil
- 3 tbsp paprika
- 1½ tbsp (25 g) butter
- 7 tbsp (100 ml) white wine
- 1⅓ cups (400 ml) light whipping cream
- 2 sprigs cilantro
- salt, freshly ground pepper

≫ Tip the linseed onto a plate.

≫ Peel and chop 1 onion. Sweat in a skillet with 1 tablespoon of the oil for 10 minutes over low heat. Add 1 tablespoon of the paprika and brown lightly for 1 minute, stirring continuously. Turn off the heat and leave to cool.

≫ In a large bowl, mix the ground beef with the sweated onion, salt, and pepper. Form into balls the size of a large walnut, roll them in the linseed, and refrigerate.

≫ Peel and slice the two remaining onions. Sweat in the butter in a casserole for 10 minutes over low heat. Add the remaining paprika and brown lightly for 1 minute, stirring continuously. Add the white wine and boil for 5 minutes. Add the cream, salt, and pepper. Mix together and cook for a further 10 minutes over low heat.

≫ Wash and chop the cilantro.

≫ In a large skillet, seal the meatballs in the remaining oil for 2 minutes on each side. Transfer to the casserole of sauce, cover, and cook for 20 minutes over low heat, removing the lid 5 minutes before the end of cooking time. Then remove the meatballs from the casserole and reduce the sauce if necessary.

≫ Sprinkle the meatballs with cilantro and serve immediately.

Serve the meatballs with basmati rice flavored with cardamom or curry.

MEATBALLS OF LAMB WITH RED CURRY, CORIANDER, AND COCONUT

PREPARATION: 40 minutes

COOKING TIME: 45 minutes

INGREDIENTS

Serves 6

- 2 lb (900 g) ground lamb
- 2 tbsp coriander seeds
- 1 small bunch fresh cilantro
- 2 large yellow onions
- 2 carrots
- 2 zucchini
- 3 tbsp flour
- 3½ tbsp (50 ml) olive oil
- 2 generous tbsp red curry paste
- 7 tbsp (100 ml) coconut milk
- 3 sprigs chervil
- salt, freshly ground pepper

≫ Crush the coriander seeds coarsely. Pick off the leaves of the fresh cilantro and chop. Peel and chop 1 onion.

≫ In a large bowl, using your hands, mix the meat with the chopped onion, fresh cilantro, coriander seeds, salt, and pepper until smooth and even. Form into balls the size of a large walnut.

≫ Peel and rinse the carrots; wash the zucchini. Cut the vegetables in chunks. Peel and slice the second onion.

≫ Roll the meatballs in the flour. In a casserole, heat the olive oil and seal the meatballs for 2–3 minutes over high heat. Reduce the heat, add the onion and sweat for 5 minutes, stirring continuously. Add the curry paste and brown lightly for 2 minutes. Add the coconut milk and enough water to cover the meatballs, and season with salt and pepper. Add the carrots, cover, and cook for 20 minutes over medium heat.

≫ Then add the zucchini to the casserole and cook for a further 20 minutes (If necessary, top up with a little water during cooking).

≫ Just before serving, sprinkle the meatballs and vegetables with chopped chervil. Eat while very hot.

MEATBALLS OF LAMB, MOROCCAN-STYLE

PREPARATION: 30 minutes
COOKING TIME: 45 minutes

INGREDIENTS

Serves 6

- 2 lb (900 g) ground lamb
  (shoulder)
- 2 tomatoes
- generous 1 lb (500 g) new carrots
- 2 yellow onions
- 1 small bunch cilantro
- 1 salted preserved lemon
- 7 tbsp (100 ml) olive oil
- 2 tbsp honey
- 1 tbsp cumin seeds
- 1 tbsp ras el hanout
- 1 tbsp harissa
- 9 tbsp (80 g) flour
- 7 oz (200 g) small black olives,
  pitted
- salt, freshly ground pepper

» Wash the tomatoes, cut in half, and remove the seeds. Roughly chop the flesh.

» Peel and rinse the carrots and cut in long sticks. Peel and chop 1 onion. Wash and chop the cilantro.

» Cut the preserved lemon in quarters, remove the seeds and flesh. Cut 1 quarter in small cubes and set the remainder aside.

» In a skillet, sweat the chopped onion in half the olive oil for 5–7 minutes over medium heat. Add the diced lemon and the honey. Mix in and cook for a further 3 minutes. Leave to cool.

» In a large bowl, mix the ground meat with the lemon mixture. Add all the spices, the harissa and the cilantro. Form into balls the size of a large walnut and roll in the flour.

» Peel and chop the second onion.

» In a casserole, seal the meatballs in the remaining olive oil for 3–4 minutes over high heat. Add the onion and fry for 3 minutes. Reduce the heat and add the 3 remaining lemon quarters, the tomato flesh and the olives.

» Add just enough cold water to cover the meatballs, then add the carrot sticks and season with salt and pepper. Cover the pan and cook for 30 minutes over medium heat. Then remove the lid and cook for a further 10–15 minutes over medium heat.

» Serve the meatballs very hot.

PREPARATION: **20 minutes**
STANDING TIME: **30 minutes**
COOKING TIME: **30 minutes**

INGREDIENTS

Serves 6

- generous 1 lb (500 g) ground shoulder of lamb
- 2 large eggplants
- coarse salt
- 10 prunes
- 6½ oz (180 g) ossau-iraty cheese
- 1 small bunch flat-leaf parsley
- 4 slices Bayonne ham
- ⅔ cup (100 g) pine nuts
- 1 level tbsp red chili pepper
- ⅔ cup (150 ml) olive oil
- salt, freshly ground pepper

Meatballs of lamb with ossau-iraty and prunes

≫ Wash the eggplant and cut in small cubes. Place in a colander with a handful of coarse salt. Weight with a plate and leave to drain for at least 30 minutes.

≫ Meanwhile, pit the prunes and cut in small pieces. Remove the crust from the cheese and cut in small cubes. Wash and chop the parsley. Cut the ham in small cubes.

≫ Grind the pine nuts, not too finely.

≫ In a large bowl, using your hands, mix the ground lamb with the prunes, parsley, cheese, ham, and red chili pepper, 3½ tablespoons of the olive oil, and salt. Form into balls the size of a large walnut, then flatten slightly to form little cakes.

≫ Pre-heat the oven to 320 °F (160 °C).

≫ Tip the ground pine nuts onto a plate and roll the meatballs in them so they are lightly coated.

≫ In a skillet, seal the meatballs in 3½ tablespoons of the remaining olive oil over high heat for 2 minutes on each side. Transfer to an oven dish with the oil they were fried in. Bake in the oven for 30 minutes.

≫ Meanwhile, drain the excess salt from the eggplant and fry in a skillet in the remaining oil for 15–20 minutes over medium heat. Season with salt and pepper.

≫ Serve the meatballs very hot with the fried eggplant.

You can replace the prunes with dried figs or dried apricots and the ossau-iraty with Emmental or Roquefort.

CRISPY MEATBALLS OF DUCK CONFIT WITH FOIE GRAS

PREPARATION: 30 minutes
COOKING TIME: 10 minutes

INGREDIENTS

Serves 6

- 4 duck legs confit
- 6 sage leaves
- 5½ oz (150 g) duck foie gras, *mi-cuit* (half-cooked)
- 1 generous tbsp thick crème fraîche
- 2 eggs
- 2 tbsp flour
- 4 oz (120 g) panko or classic breadcrumbs
- freshly ground pepper
- oil for deep frying

≫ Pre-heat the oven to 320 °F (160 °C).

≫ Chop the sage leaves.

≫ Place the duck legs in an oven dish. Heat in the oven for 10—15 minutes. Drain off the fat and leave to cool.

≫ Cut the foie gras in small cubes.

≫ De-bone the duck legs and chop the flesh. Mix in a large bowl with the sage, crème fraîche, and pepper. Form into balls the size of a large hazelnut. With your thumb, make a hole in each ball, insert 1 cube of foie gras, then reshape the balls.

≫ Beat the eggs in a deep dish. Tip the flour and breadcrumbs onto two other plates. Coat the meatballs by rolling them first in the flour, then in the egg, and finally in the breadcrumbs.

≫ Heat the frying oil to 355 °F (180 °C). Deep-fry the meatballs, in small batches, for 2—3 minutes. Drain on paper towels and serve immediately.

The meatballs can be served with black cherry jelly or a chutney and a salad of grated red cabbage.

PREPARATION: **30 minutes**
COOKING TIME: **10 minutes**

INGREDIENTS

Serves 6

- 1¼ lb (600 g) Scottish salmon fillets
  (without skin or bones)
- 1 large red onion
- 1 bunch chervil
- ½ bunch chives
- 4 sprigs cilantro
- 3 sprigs tarragon
- 2 oz (60 g) black sesame seeds
- 3 oz (80 g) white sesame seeds
- 1 generous tsp wasabi
- salt, freshly-ground pepper
- oil for deep frying

For the coconut sauce

- generous ¾ cup (200 ml) coconut milk
- 7 tbsp (100 ml) liquid cream
- ½ yellow onion
- 1 level tsp turmeric
- 2 tbsp olive oil

Fishballs of salmon with red onion and herb mikado and coconut sauce

≫ To make the fishballs: peel the red onion and chop finely. Wash and chop the herbs. Chop the salmon roughly.

≫ On a plate, mix the black and white sesame seeds.

》 In a large bowl, using your hands, mix the salmon with two-thirds of the herbs, the red onion, wasabi, salt, and pepper. Form into walnut-sized balls, roll them in the sesame seeds, and refrigerate.

》 For the sauce: peel and chop the ½ yellow onion. Sweat in a saucepan in the olive oil for 5 minutes over medium heat. Add the turmeric and brown for 2 minutes, stirring continuously. Add the coconut milk and the cream and season with salt and pepper to taste. Boil for 10 minutes. Purée the sauce and set aside.

》 Heat the frying oil to 355 °F (180 °C). Fry the salmon balls, in small batches, in the hot oil for 2–3 minutes until golden brown. Drain on paper towels.

》 Serve very hot with the remaining herbs and the coconut sauce.

FISHBALLS OF SALT COD WITH A TOMATO AND CHILI COULIS

PREPARATION: 1 hour
SOAKING: 24 hours
COOKING TIME: 45 minutes

INGREDIENTS

Serves 6

- 1¼ lb (600 g) salt cod
- generous 1 lb (500 g) potatoes
- 4 tomatoes
- 2 shallots
- 4 garlic cloves
- 7 tbsp (100 ml) olive oil
- ½ red chili
- 1 level tbsp granulated sugar
- 1 bouquet garni
- 2 cups (500 ml) milk
- 1 small bunch flat-leaf parsley
- ⅔ cup (100 g) flour
- salt, freshly ground pepper
- oil for deep frying

≫ The day before, rinse the cod under cold running water, then soak in a large bowl of cold water to remove the salt, changing the water 6 or 7 times over the 24 hours.

≫ On the day, peel and rinse the potatoes and cut in pieces. Place in a saucepan of cold salted water with 2 of the garlic cloves and boil for 20 minutes.

≫ Plunge the tomatoes in a saucepan of boiling water for 20 seconds; drain and rinse in cold water. Remove the skins and seeds and chop the flesh.

≫ De-seed the chili and chop finely. Peel and chop the shallots and the remaining garlic cloves.

≫ In a saucepan, sweat the shallots and garlic in half of the olive oil for 5 minutes over medium heat. Add the chopped tomatoes, chili, sugar, ⅔ cup (150 ml) of water, the bouquet garni, and salt and pepper to taste. Cook for 20 minutes over medium heat.

≫ In another saucepan, heat the milk with 2 cups (500 ml) of water. Rinse the cod and poach in simmering milk and water for 6–8 minutes. Drain and leave to cool.

≫ Drain the potatoes and purée with a potato masher. Wash and chop the parsley.

≫ Flake the cod, taking care to remove all the bones, and mix into the potato purée. Add the remaining oil, the parsley, and pepper to taste. Mix together until smooth and even. Form into walnut-sized balls and roll in the flour.

≫ Remove the bouquet garni from the pan of tomatoes and blend to a coulis. Keep warm.

≫ Heat the frying oil to 355 °F (180 °C) and fry the fishballs for 4–5 minutes. Drain on paper towels. Serve with the tomato and chili coulis.

FISHBALLS IN KATAIFI VERMICELLI

PREPARATION: 30 minutes

REFRIGERATION: 1 hour

COOKING TIME: 20—25 minutes

INGREDIENTS

Serves 6

- 14 oz (400 g) whiting fillets
- 7 oz (200 g) anglerfish fillets
- 7 oz (200 g) cod loin
- ½ bunch flat-leaf parsley
- 1 large shallot
- 7 tbsp (100 ml) light whipping cream
- 1 level tbsp turmeric
- 2 large pinches hot chili powder
- 7 tbsp (100 ml) olive oil
- 3 egg yolks
- 5½ oz (150 g) kataifi vermicelli
- salt, freshly ground pepper

> Wash and chop the parsley. Peel and chop the shallot.

> Remove any bones or cartilage from the fish and cut the flesh in small pieces. Place in the goblet of a food processor. Add the cream, parsley, shallot, turmeric, and chili powder, half the olive oil, salt, and pepper to taste. Blend until smooth and even. Transfer to a bowl.

> With your hands, form walnut-sized, slightly elongated balls. Arrange on a dish, cover with film and refrigerate for 1 hour.

> In a deep dish, with a fork, beat the egg yolks together with the remaining oil, 3½ tablespoons (50 ml) of cold water, salt, and pepper.

> Cut the kataifi vermicelli with scissors and put them in another plate.

> Pre-heat the oven to 390 °F (200 °C).

> Take the fishballs out of the refrigerator and roll them in the beaten egg and then in the vermicelli. Arrange on a baking sheet lined with parchment and bake in the oven for 20—25 minutes. Serve immediately with melted butter flavored with turmeric.

For a perfect fish mixture, when you have assembled it, pass it through a sieve and refrigerate for a short while.

FISHBALLS, BOUILLABAISSE-STYLE

PREPARATION: **40 minutes**

COOKING TIME: **50 minutes**

INGREDIENTS

Serves 6

- 14 oz (400 g) whiting fillets
- 7 oz (200 g) anglerfish fillets
- 6 Dublin Bay prawns
- 1 large yellow onion
- 1 medium carrot
- 7 tbsp (100 ml) olive oil
- 1 tbsp tomato paste
- generous ¾ cup (200 ml) white wine
- 3 medium shallots
- 4 sprigs tarragon
- ⅔ cup (100 g) flour
- 1¼ cups (300 ml) light whipping cream
- 24 cherry tomatoes
- salt, freshly ground pepper

» Peel the Dublin Bay prawns; crush the shells and heads.

» Peel and slice the onion and the carrot. Fry in a sauteuse pan in half the olive oil over high heat for 3 minutes. Add the shells and heads of the prawns, then the tomato paste, and brown lightly for 3 minutes, stirring continuously. Add the white wine and 1¼ cups (300 ml) of water, and cook for 30 minutes over medium heat.

» Meanwhile, peel and chop the shallots. Cut the whiting and anglerfish fillets in small pieces. Wash the tarragon and pick off the leaves.

» Place the pieces of fish, the shallots, prawn tails, tarragon, salt, and pepper, in the goblet of a food processor. Mix for 2 minutes until smooth and even. Form into balls the size of a large walnut, roll in the flour, and refrigerate.

» Add the cream to the pan, mix in, and cook for a further 15 minutes over medium heat. Mix everything together with a hand mixer. Strain this sauce and pour into a large saucepan. Check the seasoning, adding salt and pepper if necessary, then warm up over low heat.

» Heat the remaining oil in a skillet and sear the fishballs for 2 minutes over medium heat. Then add them to the sauce. Add the cherry tomatoes and simmer for 12—15 minutes over medium heat, turning the fishballs halfway through. Serve immediately.

Serve with rice or small vegetables in season (previously steamed or boiled) warmed up in the sauce.

FISHBALLS OF POLLOCK WITH OLIVES, COOKED IN A TAGINE

PREPARATION: **40 minutes**

COOKING TIME: **40 minutes**

INGREDIENTS

Serves 6

- 1¼ lb (600 g) pollock fillets
- 3 sprigs cilantro
- 1 tbsp thick crème fraîche
- ½ tsp ras el hanout
- ⅓ cup (50 g) breadcrumbs
- 5½ oz (150 g) pitted black olives
- 7 tbsp (100 ml) olive oil
- ⅓ cup (50 g flour)
- 2 zucchini
- 2 yellow onions
- 2 lemons
- Salt, freshly ground pepper

》 Remove any bones from the fish and cut in pieces. Wash the cilantro and pick off the leaves.

》 Place the pieces of fish, the crème fraîche, cilantro, ras el hanout, breadcrumbs, one-third of the olives, 2 tablespoons of olive oil, salt, and pepper in the goblet of a food processor. Blend to a smooth, even mixture. Form into balls the size of a large walnut, roll them in the flour, and refrigerate.

》 Wash the zucchini and cut in small pieces. Peel and slice the onions.

》 In a sauteuse pan, sweat the onions in 3½ tablespoons (50 ml) of olive oil for 5 minutes over medium heat. Add the zucchini and salt and pepper to taste. Mix together and cook for 8–10 minutes over medium heat. Then add the remaining olives, ⅔ cup (150 ml) of water and the lemons cut in quarters. Cook for a further 10 minutes.

》 Pre-heat the oven to 320 °F (160 °C).

》 In a skillet, seal the fish balls in the remaining olive oil for 3–4 minutes over high heat.

》 Transfer the contents of the pan to a tagine, or ovenproof dish. Arrange the fishballs on top with their cooking juices, pressing them down slightly into the vegetables. Bake in the oven for 15–20 minutes.

》 Serve immediately with rice or couscous.

Fishballs with onion and harissa purée and sweet and sour sauce

PREPARATION: **30 minutes**
COOKING TIME: **50 minutes**

INGREDIENTS

Serves 6

- 1½ lb (700 g) fillets of white fish (whiting, pollock, etc.)
- 5½ oz (150 g) smoked haddock fillet
- 2 large yellow onions
- 3½ tbsp (50 ml) olive oil
- 9 tbsp (120 g) granulated sugar
- 1 tsp ground cumin
- 1 level tbsp harissa
- 4 sprigs cilantro
- generous ¾ cup (200 ml) wine vinegar
- 7 tbsp (100 ml) fish stock
- salt, freshly ground pepper

≫ Peel and chop 1 onion. Sweat in a skillet in half the olive oil for 8–10 minutes over medium heat. Add 1½ tablespoons (20 g) of sugar, the cumin and the harissa. Brown for 5 minutes over low heat, stirring continuously. Leave to cool.

≫ Wash the cilantro and pick off the leaves. Remove any bones from the fish and cut the flesh in pieces.

≫ Place the pieces of fish in the goblet of a food processor with pepper and a little salt. Blend for 1 minute, then add the onion-and-harissa mixture and the cilantro. Blend for a further minute until smooth and even. Form into walnut-sized balls and refrigerate.

≫ Peel and chop the second onion. Place in a saucepan with the remaining sugar, the vinegar, salt, and pepper. Bring to a boil, then cook for 15 minutes over medium heat to give a fairly thick sweet and sour sauce. Add the fish stock and continue cooking for 10 minutes.

≫ Heat the remaining oil in a skillet and fry the fishballs for 6–8 minutes over medium heat, turning several times during cooking. Add the sauce to the skillet and cook for a further 6–8 minutes, basting the fishballs regularly with sauce, using a spoon.

≫ Serve immediately with a salad of red or white cabbage or with rice.

SHRIMPBALLS FLAVORED WITH ANISE

PREPARATION: 50 minutes
FREEZING: 2 hours
COOKING TIME: 15 minutes

INGREDIENTS

Serves 6

- 1¼ lb (600 g) shrimp
- 3 sprigs tarragon
- 2 cups (500 ml) milk
- 2 leaves gelatin
- 2½ tbsp (40 g) butter
- 1 cup (140 g) flour
- 2 whole eggs + 1 yolk
- ¾ cup (80 g) grated Gruyère
- 1 tbsp fennel seeds
- 2 tbsp pastis (for the anise flavor)
- 5½ oz (150 g) breadcrumbs
- oil for deep frying
- salt, freshly ground pepper

❯ Peel the shrimp (reserve the shells): you should be left with 14 oz–1 lb (400–450 g) flesh. Wash the tarragon and pick off the leaves.

❯ In a saucepan, boil the milk with the shrimp shells, salt, and pepper for 2 minutes. Turn off the heat and leave to infuse for 10 minutes. Pass the milk through a fine sieve.

❯ Soak the gelatin leaves in a bowl of cold water for 10 minutes.

❯ Melt the butter in a saucepan. Add ⅓ cup (50 g) of the flour and cook for 5 minutes over low heat, stirring continuously to give a pale roux. Add the infused milk and cook for 4–5 minutes over medium heat while continuing to stir to make a béchamel. Remove from the heat, mix in the egg yolk, the softened gelatin, and the grated cheese. Ensure gelatin has dissolved. Leave to cool.

❯ Place the shrimp flesh in the blender goblet. Add the fennel seeds, tarragon leaves, pastis, and salt and pepper to taste. Blend for 2 minutes. Mix this shrimp purée with the béchamel.

❯ Transfer the shrimp mixture to a piping bag with a large, plain nozzle and pipe walnut-sized balls on a baking sheet lined with parchment. Place in the freezer for 2 hours.

❯ Beat the whole eggs in a deep dish. Tip the remaining flour and the breadcrumbs onto another two plates. Roll the balls in the flour, then in the beaten egg, and finally in the breadcrumbs.

❯ Heat the frying oil to 355 °F (180 °C). Deep-fry the shrimp balls, in small batches, in the hot oil for 2–3 minutes until golden brown. Drain on paper towels. Sprinkle with salt and serve immediately.

Serve with fried parsley and lemon or lime quarters.

SHRIMPBALLS WITH CURRY AND COCONUT MILK

PREPARATION: **45 minutes**
COOKING TIME: **45 minutes**

INGREDIENTS

Serves 6

- 14 oz (400 g) large, uncooked shrimp, fresh or frozen
- 14 oz (400) g whiting fillets (boneless)
- 2 medium yellow onions
- ⅓ cup (80 ml) olive oil
- 2 tbsp curry powder
- 3½ tbsp (50 ml) fish stock
- 1¼ cups (300 ml) coconut milk
- 3½ tbsp (50 ml) liquid cream
- 3 sprigs cilantro
- salt, freshly ground pepper

> Peel the shrimp completely, reserving the shells.

> Cut the whiting and shrimp in small pieces.

> Peel and chop 1 onion. Sweat in a skillet in half the olive oil for 3 minutes over low heat. Add the pieces of shrimp, 1 tablespoon of the curry powder, and salt and pepper to taste. Brown for 3 minutes over high heat, stirring continuously. Turn off the heat and leave to cool.

> Put the pieces of whiting in a blender goblet. Add the contents of the skillet, 7 tablespoons (100 ml) of the coconut milk, salt, and pepper. Blend for 1–2 minutes until smooth and even. Form into walnut-sized balls and refrigerate.

> Peel and slice the second onion. Sweat in a large saucepan with the remaining oil for 3 minutes over medium heat. Add the shrimp shells and the second tablespoon of curry powder. Mix in and brown for 2 minutes over high heat. Add the fish stock and bring to a boil. Add the remaining coconut milk and the cream, season with salt and pepper, and cook for 20 minutes over medium heat. Mix everything together using a hand mixer. Strain the sauce and pour into a sauteuse pan. Bring to a boil and season again with salt and pepper if necessary.

> Place the shrimpballs carefully in the sauce and turn down the heat. Cook for 15–20 minutes, turning halfway through.

> Serve very hot with the sauce, sprinkled with roughly chopped cilantro.

CRISPY RICEBALLS WITH GORGONZOLA AND INK

PREPARATION: **40 minutes**
REFRIGERATION: **3 hours**
COOKING TIME: **30 minutes**

INGREDIENTS

Serves 6

- generous ¾ cup (160 g) arborio or round-grain rice
- 2½ cups (600 ml) chicken stock
- 1 yellow onion
- 3½ tbsp (50 ml) olive oil
- 7 tbsp (100 ml) white wine
- 1 tbsp squid ink
- 3½ tbsp (50 g) butter
- 5½ oz (150 g) Gorgonzola
- 2 eggs
- ⅔ cup (90 g) flour
- 1 cup (120 g) breadcrumbs
- oil for deep frying
- salt, freshly ground pepper

≫ Heat the chicken stock in a saucepan.

≫ Peel and chop the onion. Sweat in a saucepan with the olive oil for 2 minutes over medium heat. Add the rice and stir over low heat to coat with the oil. Add the white wine and season with salt and pepper. Reduce the wine over high heat for 4–5 minutes, then add the hot stock in single tablespoons, as the rice absorbs it. Reckon on 18 minutes for perfect cooking. Halfway through, add the squid ink to the pan. When the rice is cooked, turn off the heat and mix in the butter in pieces. Transfer the risotto to a dish and leave to cool. Then cut the Gorgonzola in pieces and mix in. Allow to cool completely and refrigerate the risotto for 2 hours to set firm.

≫ Form the cold, compacted risotto into balls the size of a large walnut.

≫ Beat the eggs in a deep dish. Tip the flour and breadcrumbs onto two plates. Roll the balls of risotto first in the flour, then in the beaten egg and lastly in the breadcrumbs. Refrigerate again for 1 hour.

≫ Heat the frying oil to 355 °F (180 °C). Deep-fry the riceballs in the hot oil for a few seconds until golden, then drain on paper towels and serve immediately.

You can serve these riceballs with a Gorgonzola cream. In a saucepan, bring 2 cups (500 ml) light whipping cream to a boil; add 3½ oz (100 g) Gorgonzola cut in pieces, and beat in with a hand whisk; season with salt and pepper to taste.

POTATO BALLS WITH EMMENTAL

PREPARATION: 30 minutes
COOKING TIME: 15 minutes

INGREDIENTS

Serves 6

- 1¾ lb (750 g) small, firm potatoes
- 2 cups (220 g) grated Emmental cheese
- 2 egg yolks
- ½ tsp grated nutmeg
- 2 tbsp flour
- salt, freshly ground pepper
- oil for deep frying

> Peel the potatoes, to give 1¼ lb (600 g) net. Rinse, then grate finely with a mandoline.

> Place the grated potatoes, cheese, egg yolks, nutmeg, salt, and pepper in a large bowl. Mix by hand until smooth and even. Form into balls the size of a large walnut, pressing hard to squeeze as much water as possible out of the potatoes.

> Roll the balls in the flour. Heat the frying oil to 355 °F (180 °C). Deep-fry the potato balls in small batches for 4–5 minutes. Drain on paper towels.

> Serve very hot with black cherry or fig jelly, or chutney.

You can replace the Emmental with Comté, Appenzeller, ossau-iraty or mimolette vieille.

EGGPLANT BALLS WITH COUSCOUS

PREPARATION: **40 minutes**
STANDING TIME: **1 hour**
COOKING TIME: **25 minutes**

INGREDIENTS

Serves 6

- 14 oz (400 g) eggplant
- 1 tbsp coarse salt
- ¾–1 cup (150 g) wheat couscous, medium or finely ground
- ⅔ cup (150 ml) olive oil
- ¾ cup (80 g) breadcrumbs
- ¾ cup (100 g) poppy seeds
- 3 sprigs chervil
- 1 large bunch round radishes
- 3½ tbsp (50 ml) lemon juice
- salt, freshly ground pepper
- oil for deep frying

≫ Wash the eggplant and cut in small cubes. Place in a colander and sprinkle with the coarse salt. Cover with a small plate and leave to drain for 1 hour.

≫ In a large bowl, mix the couscous with 3 tablespoons of the olive oil and pepper to taste. Add boiling water to cover. Cover the bowl with a cloth or a plate and leave for 15 minutes for the couscous to swell.

≫ Shake the eggplant to remove the excess salt. Cook in a skillet in ¼–⅓ cup (60–80 ml) of the olive oil for 10–15 minutes over medium heat, stirring continuously. Season with pepper and leave to cool.

≫ Break up the couscous with a fork or by hand. Mix with the eggplant, breadcrumbs, and 2 tablespoons of poppy seeds. Form into balls the size of a large walnut, pressing firmly with your hands, roll in the remaining poppy seeds, and refrigerate.

≫ Wash the chervil and pick off the leaves. Wash and trim the radishes and cut in quarters. Place in a large bowl. Flavor with the remaining oil, the lemon juice, salt, and pepper. Add the chervil leaves and mix together.

≫ At the last moment, heat the frying oil to 355 °F (180 °C). Carefully fry the balls of eggplant, in small batches, for 1 minute. Drain on paper towels.

≫ Serve very hot with the radish and lemon salad.

FALAFELS

PREPARATION: **45 minutes**
SOAKING: **12 hours**
COOKING TIME: **15 minutes**

INGREDIENTS

Serves 6

- 1¼ cups (250 g) dried chickpeas
- 3 garlic cloves
- 1 small yellow onion
- 1 small bunch flat-leaf parsley
- 1 small bunch cilantro
- 3 tbsp sesame seeds
- 1 tsp chili powder
- ⅓ cup (80 ml) olive oil
- oil for deep frying
- salt, freshly ground pepper

> The day before, soak the chickpeas in a large bowl of cold water for 12 hours.

> On the day, rinse the chickpeas several times under cold running water and drain completely in a sieve.

> Peel and chop the garlic cloves and the onion. Wash and chop the parsley and the cilantro.

> Place the chickpeas in a blender goblet and purée for 3 minutes. Add the onion, garlic, sesame seeds, herbs, chili powder, olive oil, and salt and pepper to taste. Blend for a further 3–4 minutes to a smooth paste. Form into walnut-sized balls and flatten slightly.

> Heat the frying oil to 355 °F (180 °C). Deep-fry the falafels in small batches for 4–5 minutes until golden brown. Drain on paper towels.

> Serve the falafels in buckwheat pancakes with sliced onion, salad and cottage cheese with herbs.

Chocolate balls

PREPARATION: **45 minutes**

REFRIGERATION: **6 hours**

FREEZING: **4 hours**

COOKING TIME: **5 minutes**

INGREDIENTS

Serves 6

- 14 oz (400 g) dark baking chocolate
- 3½ tbsp (50 ml) light whipping cream
- ½ tsp powdered cardamom or 3 pinches cinnamon
- 3 eggs
- 7 tbsp (60 g) flour
- 4 oz (120 g) breadcrumbs, panko or classic
- ⅔ cup (60 g) grated coconut
- 3½ tbsp (50 g) sugar
- oil for frying

> Chop the chocolate with a knife and place the pieces in a large bowl.

> In a saucepan, bring the cream to a boil with the cardamom (or cinnamon). Pour the boiling cream over the chopped chocolate and leave to stand for 5 minutes. Then beat together for 8–10 minutes to give a smooth, airy ganache. Cover with plastic film and refrigerate for 6 hours.

> Beat the eggs in a deep dish. Tip the flour onto a plate. On another plate, mix together the breadcrumbs, grated coconut, and sugar.

> Take the ganache out of the refrigerator and, with your hands, form 18 walnut-sized balls of chocolate. Put them in the freezer for 15 minutes. Then roll them first in the flour, then in the beaten egg, and lastly in the breadcrumb mixture. Coat them a second time by rolling them only in the beaten egg and the breadcrumb mixture. Freeze for 3–4 hours.

> At the last moment, heat the frying oil to 355 °F (180 °C). Fry the frozen balls in small batches for 30 seconds, then drain on paper towels.

> Serve immediately at coffee time or as a dessert with a coulis (e.g. orange, passion fruit, raspberry, or mango).

SWEET RICEBALLS WITH A MANGO AND COCONUT COULIS

PREPARATION: **45 minutes**
REFRIGERATION: **3 hours**
COOKING TIME: **50 minutes**

INGREDIENTS

Serves 6

- ⅔ cup (120 g) round-grain rice
- 1 vanilla bean
- 6 tbsp (90 ml) milk
- 7 tbsp (100 ml) coconut milk
- 9 tbsp (120 g) granulated sugar
- 2 eggs
- 2 oz (60 g) breadcrumbs, panko or classic
- generous ¾ cup (80 g) grated coconut
- ⅓ cup (50 g) flour
- oil for deep frying

For the coulis
- 1 very ripe mango
- 7 tbsp (100 ml) coconut milk
- 4½ tbsp (60 g) granulated sugar

≫ Rinse the rice in a sieve under cold running water. Split the vanilla bean open lengthways and scrape out the seeds with the blade of a knife.

≫ In a saucepan, bring the milk to a boil with the coconut milk and vanilla seeds. Add the rice and cook for 30 minutes over very low heat, stirring regularly. Stir in the sugar and cook for a further 10–15 minutes over low heat, stirring continuously. Transfer the rice to a container and leave to cool. Refrigerate for at least 2 hours to set firm.

≫ Beat the eggs in a deep dish. Mix the breadcrumbs with the grated coconut on a plate. Tip the flour onto another plate.

≫ Form the hardened rice into balls the size of a large hazelnut. Roll in the flour, then in the beaten egg, and lastly in the coconut-and-breadcrumb mixture. Refrigerate for 1 hour.

≫ To make the coulis: in a saucepan, boil the coconut milk with the sugar and 7 tablespoons (100 ml) of water. Leave to cool. Peel the mango and cut the flesh in small pieces. Transfer to a deep container with the sweetened coconut milk and mix to a coulis using a hand mixer. Strain and refrigerate.

≫ At the last moment, heat the frying oil to 355 °F (180 °C). Fry the riceballs in small batches for 30 seconds. Drain on paper towels.

≫ Serve warm with the cold mango coulis.

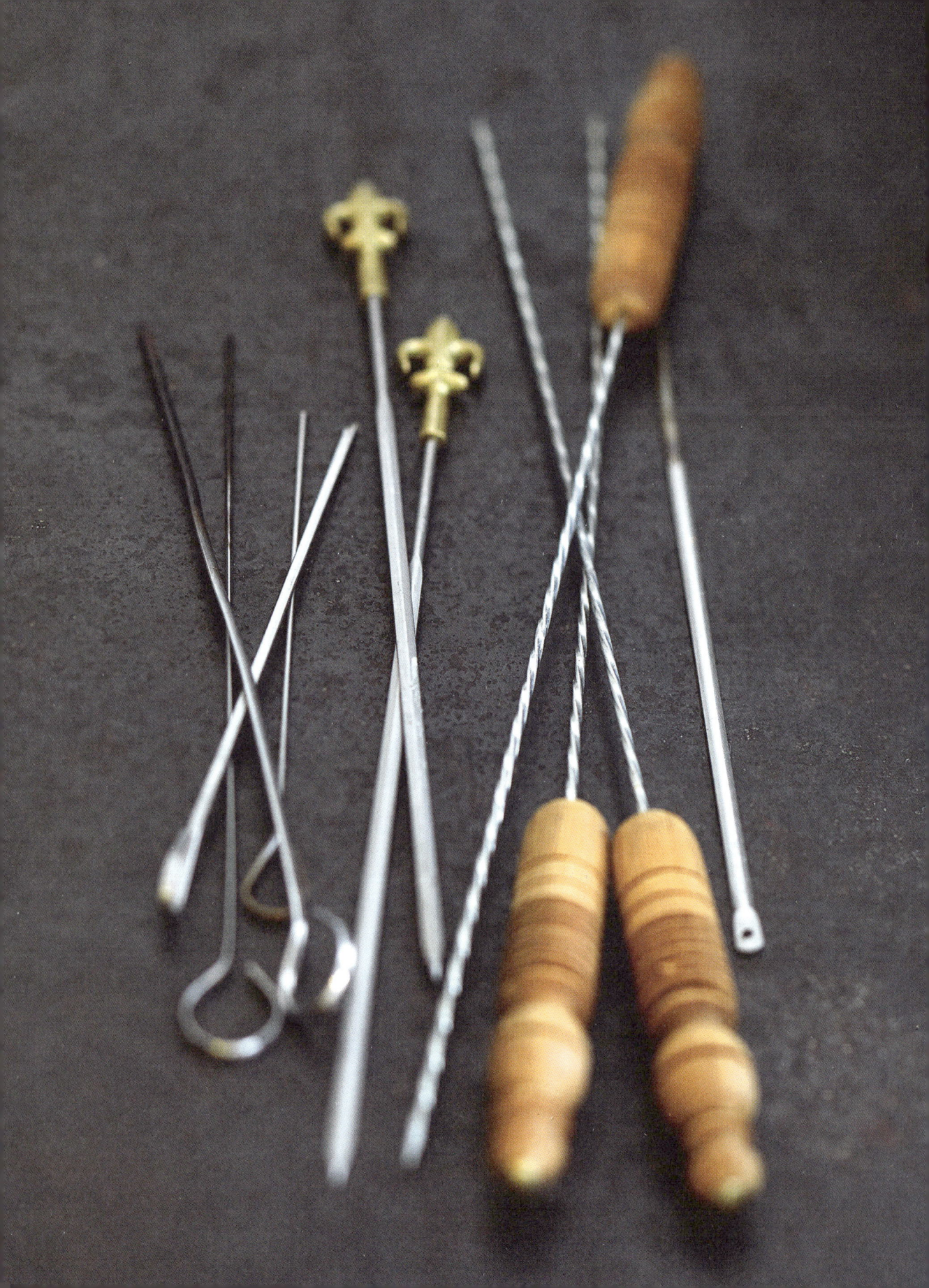

SKEWERS

Skewers of tender caramelized chicken with ginger

PREPARATION: **20 minutes**
MARINATING: **6 hours**
COOKING TIME: **15 minutes**

INGREDIENTS

Serves 6

- 6 chicken breasts
- 2 oz (60 g) fresh ginger
- 2 garlic cloves
- 2 large lemons
- 3 tbsp liquid honey
- 3 tbsp nuoc nam
- 3½ tbsp (50 ml) rice vinegar
- 3½ tbsp (50 ml) olive oil
- salt, freshly ground pepper

≫ Peel and grate the ginger. Peel the garlic cloves and reduce to a purée.

≫ Squeeze the lemons and strain the juice. Pour into a large bowl. Add the ginger, garlic, honey, nuoc nam, rice vinegar, salt, and pepper, and beat together.

≫ Cut the chicken breasts in small cubes. Transfer to the bowl and mix everything together by hand so the chicken is well covered with the marinade. Cover the bowl with plastic film and refrigerate for 6 hours.

≫ Drain the chicken cubes (reserving the marinade) and thread on wooden skewers.

≫ Heat the oil in a large skillet. Place the skewers in the pan and cook for 5 minutes on each side over medium heat. Then add the marinade to the skillet, turn up the heat and cook for a further 5 minutes to slightly caramelize the skewers.

≫ Serve immediately with couscous with raisins, flavored with ground ginger.

SKEWERS OF TANDOORI CHICKEN

PREPARATION: 20 minutes
MARINATING: 12 hours
COOKING TIME: 40 minutes

INGREDIENTS

Serves 6

- 6 chicken breasts
- 1¾ oz (50 g) fresh ginger
- 6 garlic cloves
- 2 lemons
- 1 lime
- 1 medium yellow onion
- 4 creamy natural plain yogurts (total 500 g)
- 2 tbsp tandoori spices
- 3½ tbsp (50 ml) sunflower oil
- ½ bunch fresh mint
- salt, freshly ground pepper

>> The previous day, peel and grate the ginger. Peel and chop 4 garlic cloves. Squeeze the juice out of the lemons and the lime. Peel the onion and chop finely. Cut the chicken breasts in small cubes.

>> In a large bowl, mix half the yogurt with the ground tandoori spices, the onion, garlic, ginger, oil, lemon and lime juice, salt, and pepper. Add the cubes of chicken and mix in so they are thoroughly coated. Cover the bowl with plastic film and marinate in the refrigerator for 12 hours.

>> On the day, pre-heat the oven to 340 °F (170 °C).

>> Drain the chicken cubes and thread on wooden skewers. Place the skewers on a baking sheet lined with parchment and bake in the oven for 35—40 minutes until golden brown.

>> Meanwhile, peel and chop the remaining garlic cloves. Wash the mint and chop the leaves. In a bowl, mix remaining yogurt with the mint and the garlic. Keep this sauce in the refrigerator.

>> Serve the skewers very hot with the yogurt sauce, accompanied by pita bread and salad or fried cardamom rice.

SKEWERS OF DUCK FILLET WITH ORANGE

PREPARATION: **20 minutes**
COOKING TIME: **20 minutes**

INGREDIENTS

Serves 6

- 24 duck breast fillets
- generous 1 lb (500 g) oyster mushrooms
- 2 large shallots
- 4 blood oranges
- ¼ cup (60 g) butter
- 3 tbsp olive oil
- 2 tbsp grenadine syrup
- 2 generous tbsp liquid honey
- salt, freshly ground pepper

≫ Wash the oyster mushrooms briefly under cool running water, pat dry, and cut in pieces. Peel and chop the shallots.

≫ Reserve the zest from 2 oranges. Reserve the juice from 3 oranges and cut the fourth in 6 segments.

≫ In a skillet, sweat the shallots in the butter for 3 minutes over low heat. Add the oyster mushrooms and cook for 5–8 minutes over medium heat, stirring continuously. Season with salt and pepper to taste. Turn off the heat.

≫ Thread 2 pieces of duck breast fillet on each wooden skewer. Season with salt and pepper. In a skillet, seal the skewers of duck in the olive oil for 2 minutes on each side over high heat. Transfer to a plate.

≫ Degrease the pan, then add the grenadine syrup and honey. Caramelize lightly over high heat. Add the orange juice and season with salt and pepper. Reduce for a few minutes over high heat to give a syrupy sauce.

≫ Return the skewers to the pan, along with the orange segments. Heat for 3–4 minutes, rolling the skewers and using a spoon to coat them with sauce.

≫ Warm up the mushrooms over low heat.

≫ Serve the skewers with the mushrooms, the orange segments, and the sauce.

SKEWERS OF DUCK BREAST WITH BLACK SESAME, FENNEL, AND BABY POTATOES

PREPARATION: **30 minutes**
MARINATING: **1 hour**
COOKING TIME: **50 minutes**

INGREDIENTS

Serves 6

- 3 duck breasts
- 4 generous tbsp liquid honey
- 7 tbsp (100 ml) rice vinegar
- 2 tbsp sesame oil
- generous 1 lb (500 g) baby potatoes
- 2 fennel bulbs
- 3½ tbsp (50 ml) olive oil
- ⅓ cup (80 g) butter
- 3 oz (80 g) black sesame seeds
- salt, freshly ground pepper

≫ Remove a little of the fat from the duck breasts with a small kitchen knife and cut in large cubes.

≫ In a saucepan, warm the honey and the rice vinegar. Remove from the heat, add the sesame oil, salt, and pepper.

≫ Thread the cubes of duck on wooden skewers. Place the skewers in a deep dish and pour over the honey marinade. Cover the dish with plastic film and marinate for 1 hour in the refrigerator.

≫ Wash the potatoes and boil in their skins for 15 minutes in a saucepan (starting with cold water).

≫ Wash the fennel bulbs (removing the outer leaves if necessary) and cut them in 6 segments. Brown lightly in a sauteuse pan in half the olive oil and half the butter for 5 minutes over medium heat. Reduce the heat, then fill two-thirds of the way with water. Season with salt and pepper. Cover with a sheet of parchment and cook for 20 minutes over medium heat.

≫ Drain the potatoes and fry lightly in a skillet in the remaining butter and oil for 5–8 minutes over medium heat. Season with salt and pepper.

≫ Drain the skewers, reserving the marinade, and toast in a hot dry skillet for 2–3 minutes on each side. Turn them out onto a plate. Add a little of the marinade to the skillet and reduce over high heat. Return the skewers to the skillet, sprinkle with sesame seeds and roll rapidly in the sauce to coat them thoroughly.

≫ Serve the skewers and their sauce with the braised fennel and the potatoes.

SKEWERS OF BEEF MARINATED IN THAI BASIL AND SOY SAUCE

PREPARATION: **15 minutes**

MARINATING: **4 hours**

COOKING TIME:

about 5 minutes

INGREDIENTS

Serves 6

- 2 lb (900 g) beef (rump steak)
- 1 chilicote
- 2 garlic cloves
- 2 oz (60 g) fresh ginger root
- 12 leaves Thai basil
- ⅓ cup (75 ml) of olive oil
- 3½ tbsp (50 ml) de vinegar de rice
- ⅔ cup (150 ml) soy sauce
- 3 tbsp nuoc nam
- salt, freshly-ground pepper
- 3 tbsp liquid honey

> Wash, seed and chop the chilicote. Peel and chop the garlic cloves. Peel and grate the ginger. Wash and chop the basil.

> Cut the meat in ⅓ inch (1 cm) cubes.

> In a large bowl, mix together the chilicote, garlic, ginger, and basil. Add 3½ tablespoons (50 ml) of oil, the rice vinegar, the soy sauce, nuoc nam, salt, and pepper. Add the cubes of meat to the bowl and mix with your hands so the meat is thoroughly coated in the marinade. Cover the bowl with plastic film and refrigerate for 4 hours.

> Thread the marinated meat cubes on the wooden skewers.

> Heat the remaining oil in a large skillet over medium heat, add the honey, and fry the skewers for 1 to 3 minutes on each side (until done as desired). They should be slightly caramelized.

> Serve the skewers with asparagus and braised cherry tomatoes.

These skewers are also delicious if cooked on a cooking plate or a barbecue.

MINI-SKEWERS OF BEEF WITH CHEESE AND TERIYAKI SAUCE

PREPARATION: **20 minutes**
COOKING TIME: **10 minutes**

INGREDIENTS

Serves 6

- 18 thin slices beef for carpaccio
  (ask your butcher to slice the beef
  really thinly)
- 9 slices cheddar for burgers
- 3 tbsp sunflower oil
- ⅔ cup (150 ml) teriyaki sauce
- salt, freshly ground pepper

≫ Cut the cheese slices in half.

≫ Place the slices of meat on the worktop and season with salt and pepper. Place half a slice of cheese at one end of each slice of meat and fasten with a wooden toothpick. Roll up carefully, pressing the meat firmly to hold the toothpick in place.

≫ Heat the oil in a skillet and seal the skewers for 3–4 minutes over high heat, turning several times during cooking so they brown nicely. Then pour over the teriyaki sauce and cook for 4–5 minutes, rolling the skewers around in the skillet so they are lightly coated. Serve immediately.

Serve with fregola pasta and sliced chives, rice, or vegetable tempuras.

Skewers of beef and potatoes with peppercorns

PREPARATION: **30 minutes**
COOKING TIME: **40 minutes**

INGREDIENTS

Serves 6

- 2–2¼ lb (900 g–1 kg) of prime beef
- 24 small Ratte potatoes (firm and waxy)
- 3 oz (80 g) coarsely ground dried green peppercorns
- 1¾ lb (800 g) kale leaves
- generous ¾ cup (200 ml) port
- 5½–7 tbsp (80–100 ml) cognac
- 1¼ cups (300 ml) strong veal stock
- 2 tbsp thick crème fraîche
- 4 tbsp (60 g) butter
- 2 tbsp sunflower oil
- salt, freshly ground pepper

≫ Wash the potatoes. Boil in their skins in a saucepan of salted water (starting with cold water) for 18–20 minutes. Drain and rinse under cold water.

≫ Cut the meat in cubes.

≫ Thread meat cubes and potatoes alternately on the skewers. Sprinkle the meat with half the ground green peppercorns and refrigerate.

≫ Wash the kale leaves and cook for 5–6 minutes in a large saucepan of boiling salted water (they should remain slightly crunchy). Drain and rinse under cold water.

≫ In a dry saucepan, toast the remaining ground peppercorns for 2 minutes over high heat. Add the cognac, flambé, then reduce by two-thirds. Add the port and reduce by two-thirds again to produce a syrupy consistency. Then add the veal stock, season with salt, and reduce again. Lastly, beat in the crème fraîche with a hand whisk. Mix together with a hand mixer and keep the sauce warm.

≫ Reheat the kale leaves in a skillet with the butter over medium heat. Season with salt and pepper.

≫ Salt the skewers, then cook under a very hot broiler or in a skillet with the sunflower oil for 3–4 minutes over high heat, turning regularly. Serve with the kale and cover both with the sauce.

SKEWERS OF BEEF KOFTA WITH CHILI AND RED ONION

PREPARATION: 30 minutes
COOKING TIME: 15 minutes

INGREDIENTS

Serves 6

- 1¾–2 lb (800–900 g) ground beef
- 1 large red onion
- 2 red chilis
- 1 small bunch flat-leaf parsley
- 1 pinch harissa
- 1 tsp ground cumin
- 3½ tbsp (50 ml) sunflower oil
- 1 small bunch mint
- 6½ oz (180 g) fromage blanc
- salt, freshly ground pepper

≫ Peel and chop the onion. Trim and de-seed the chilis and cut in large pieces. Wash the parsley and pick off the leaves.

≫ Put the onion, parsley, chilis, harissa, cumin, half the oil, salt, and pepper in the blender goblet. Blend for 2 minutes to produce a mixture that is not too smooth.

≫ Pre-heat the oven grill to 390 °F (200 °C).

≫ In a large bowl, using your hands, mix the ground beef with the chili mixture. Make balls of meat the size of a large walnut, then shape the koftas by pressing the meat around wooden skewers.

≫ Place the koftas on a baking sheet lined with parchment and baste with the remaining oil. Cook under the broiler for 12–15 minutes, turning halfway through.

≫ Meanwhile, wash and chop the mint. In a bowl, mix with the fromage blanc, salt, and pepper.

≫ Serve the koftas immediately with the cottage cheese sauce, accompanied by a crunchy salad or a tomato and onion salad.

SKEWERS OF PORK AND PINEAPPLE WITH HONEY

PREPARATION: 30 minutes

MARINATING: 1 hour

COOKING TIME: 50 minutes

INGREDIENTS

Serves 6

- 2 pork steaks, total weight 2 lb (900 g)
- 1 small Victoria pineapple
- 3½ tbsp (50 ml) olive oil
- 3 generous tbsp liquid honey
- 3½ tbsp (50 ml) rice vinegar
- 3½ tbsp (50 ml) pineapple juice
- 3 tbsp mustard seeds
- salt, freshly ground pepper

> Trim the pork steaks (remove any fat) and cut in approximately ¾-inch (1.5-cm) cubes.

> Remove the skin and eyes of the pineapple and cut in cubes of the same size as the meat.

> Thread alternate cubes of pork and pineapple on wooden skewers. Season with salt and pepper. Seal in the olive oil in a large skillet over high heat for 3–4 minutes on each side. Then reduce the heat and cover with the honey. Caramelize lightly for 3–4 minutes, turning them in the honey so they are well coated. Transfer the skewers to a plate.

> Turn up the heat under the skillet and add the vinegar and pineapple juice. Season with salt and pepper and add the mustard seeds. Reduce over high heat to give a syrupy sauce. Then reduce the heat, return the skewers to the skillet and warm up for 4–5 minutes over low heat, rolling them in the sauce. Serve very hot.

Serve the skewers with Brussels sprouts (cooked for 8–10 minutes in boiling salted water, then fried in butter for 5 minutes). You can replace the pineapple juice with orange juice.

Skewers of bacon coated with vinegar and sesame

PREPARATION: 30 minutes

COOKING TIME: 1 hour

INGREDIENTS

Serves 6

- 6 slices uncooked, smoked bacon, ⅝ in (1.5 cm) thick
- 1¼ lb (600 g) carrots of various colors
- 7 tbsp (100 ml) olive oil
- 7 tbsp (100 ml) red wine vinegar
- 4½ tbsp (60 g) granulated sugar
- 2 tbsp soy sauce
- 1¾ oz (50 g) golden sesame seeds
- salt, freshly ground pepper

》 Pre-heat the oven to 355 °F (180 °C).

》 Peel and rinse the carrots, then cut in four lengthways and place in an oven dish. Drizzle with two-thirds of the olive oil and season with salt and pepper. Pour a small glass of water into the bottom of the dish. Cook in the oven for 30 minutes, turning the carrots halfway through.

》 Remove any rind from the bacon and thread each slice on a wooden skewer.

》 In a small saucepan, boil the vinegar, sugar, soy sauce, salt, and pepper for 2 minutes.

》 Heat the remaining oil in a large skillet over medium heat. Add the skewers of bacon and brown lightly for 5 minutes. Turn and brown on the other side for 5 minutes. Add a little of the vinegar mixture to the skillet and continue cooking over low heat until the liquid has been reduced and the bacon is slightly caramelized. Turn the skewers over, add a little more of the vinegar mixture, and cook over low heat. Continue in the same way until all the vinegar has been used up, turning the skewers over each time to coat them. Sprinkle with sesame seeds 5 minutes before the end of cooking time.

》 Remove the roasted carrots from the oven (they should still be slightly firm) and serve them with the bacon skewers.

SKEWERS OF LAMB AND MERGUEZ SAUSAGE, ASIAN-STYLE

PREPARATION: **30 minutes**

MARINATING: **6 hours**

COOKING TIME: **15 minutes**

INGREDIENTS

Serves 6

- 1¼–1½ lb (600–700 g) lamb, leg or shoulder
- 4 sprigs fresh cilantro
- 3½ tbsp (50 ml) lemon juice
- 2 tsp cumin seeds
- 1 tsp ground coriander
- 1 tbsp harissa
- 7 tbsp (100 ml) olive oil
- 6 merguez (spicy lamb) sausages
- 1 large yellow onion
- salt, freshly ground pepper

❯ Remove the fat from the lamb and cut the meat in small cubes.

❯ Wash and chop the cilantro.

❯ In a large bowl, mix the lemon juice with the chopped cilantro, cumin, ground coriander, harissa, salt, and pepper. Stir in the olive oil with a hand whisk. Add the cubes of meat to the bowl and mix with your hands so that the meat is well coated. Cover the bowl with plastic film and marinate for 6 hours in the refrigerator.

❯ Cut the sausages in small chunks.

❯ Peel the onion and cut in pieces of the same size as the meat.

❯ Thread alternating cubes of marinated lamb, chunks of sausage, and pieces of onion on wooden skewers. Cook the skewers on a barbecue, on a cooking plate, or in a skillet for about 15 minutes, brushing with the marinade and turning regularly during cooking.

❯ Serve very hot with a salad of red onions and cilantro, grilled zucchini or couscous.

SKEWERS OF SMOKED FISH, WITH WASABI-FLAVORED AVOCADO CREAM

PREPARATION: **40 minutes**
MARINATING: **6 hours**
COOKING TIME: **5 minutes**

INGREDIENTS

Serves 6

- 11 oz (300 g) smoked haddock
- 7 oz (200 g) smoked herring
- 7 oz (200 g) smoked eel
- 2 shallots
- generous ¾ cup (200 ml) rice vinegar
- 2 tbsp (30 g) granulated sugar
- 2 tbsp (30 g) brown sugar
- 4 juniper berries
- salt, freshly ground pepper

For the avocado cream

- 3 limes
- 3½ tbsp (50 ml) liquid cream
- 1 tsp wasabi
- 3½ tbsp (50 ml) olive oil
- salt
- 2 large avocados

≫ Peel and chop the shallots. Pour the vinegar into a saucepan. Add the granulated sugar, brown sugar, juniper berries, shallots, pepper, and a pinch of salt. Boil for 5 minutes over medium heat.

≫ Remove the bones from the smoked fish. Cut the flesh in equal-sized pieces.

≫ Thread the different pieces of fish alternately on wooden skewers. Place them in a deep dish and pour over the marinade. Cover with plastic film and refrigerate for 6 hours.

≫ For the avocado cream: squeeze the limes and strain the juice. In a small saucepan, warm the cream with the wasabi, olive oil, and salt. Peel the avocados and remove the pits. Cut the flesh in small pieces. Place in a deep container with the lime juice and the wasabi cream. Mix together with a hand mixer for 2–3 minutes to give a smooth cream. Cover the avocado cream with plastic film and refrigerate until it is time to serve.

≫ Eat the skewers well chilled with the avocado cream. Serve with blinis or toast.

SKEWERS OF SMOKED HADDOCK IN A CITRUS FRUIT MARINADE WITH A SALAD OF ROOT VEGETABLES

PREPARATION: **30 minutes**
MARINATING: **2 hours**
NO COOKING

INGREDIENTS

Serves 6

- 1¾–2 lb (800–900 g) thick smoked haddock fillets
- 2 lemons
- 3 oranges (preferably blood oranges)
- 1 grapefruit
- 2 sprigs dill
- 1 tsp mild mustard
- 7 tbsp (100 ml) olive oil
- 14 oz (400 g) carrots of various colors: purple, white, orange
- 1 small beet
- salt, freshly ground pepper

> Squeeze the lemons.

> Zest 1 orange. Remove the peel and pith of all the oranges and the grapefruit and carefully extract the segments from the membranes, using a sharp knife held over a container. Set aside. Squeeze the remaining flesh to extract the juice.

> Wash the dill and chop roughly.

> In a large bowl, mix the juice of the oranges, lemon, and grapefruit with the orange zest, mustard, salt, and pepper. Beat in the olive oil and then the dill.

> Remove the skin and bones from the smoked haddock and cut the flesh in cubes. Thread these on wooden skewers. Place the skewers in a deep dish and pour over half the marinade. Cover the dish with plastic film and refrigerate for 2 hours, turning the skewers over after 1 hour in the marinade.

> Peel and rinse the carrots and beet and cut in thin strips using a mandoline. Place these in a large bowl of cold water with a handful of ice cubes, and refrigerate.

> When it is time to serve, drain the vegetables. Mix them in a serving dish with the segments of citrus fruit and flavor with the remaining marinade.

> Serve the smoked haddock skewers and vegetable strips with slices of toast.

SKEWERS OF TUNA WITH VIRGIN DRESSING AND PRESERVED LEMON

PREPARATION: 30 minutes
MARINATING: 2 hours
COOKING TIME: 25 minutes

INGREDIENTS

Serves 6

- 2¼ lb (1 kg) tuna fillets
- 5 medium tomatoes
- 3 shallots
- 1 small bunch cilantro
- ½ preserved salted lemon
- generous ¾ cup (200 ml) olive oil
- 2 small yellow zucchini
- 1 large fennel bulb
- salt, freshly ground pepper

> Plunge 2 tomatoes in a saucepan of boiling water for 30 seconds; drain and rinse under cold running water. Peel, de-seed, and cut the flesh in small cubes.

> Peel the shallots and chop finely. Wash and chop the cilantro. Cut the preserved lemon in small cubes.

> In a large bowl, mix the tomato and lemon cubes, the shallots and the cilantro. Add salt, pepper, and ½–⅔ cup (120–150 ml) of olive oil. Mix together and refrigerate this virgin dressing for 2 hours.

> Cut the tuna in ⅝–¾-inch (1.5–2-cm) cubes, then thread them on wooden skewers. Brush the skewers with olive oil and refrigerate.

> Wash the zucchini and cut in rounds ¼ inch (5 mm) thick. Wash the fennel (removing the outer leaves if necessary) and cut in very thin slices. Wash the remaining tomatoes, remove the stalk ends, and cut in two horizontally.

> Heat the broiler or a cooking plate over medium heat, and cook the fennel for 6–8 minutes on each side, the zucchini for 5–6 minutes, and the tomatoes for 3–4 minutes. Remove the vegetables from the heat, season with salt and pepper to taste, and drizzle with the remaining olive oil.

> Place the skewers under the broiler (or on a cooking plate) and cook for 5–6 minutes, turning halfway through; season with salt and pepper. Serve immediately with the broiled vegetables and covered with the virgin dressing.

Skewers of swordfish with green chili

PREPARATION: **30 minutes**
MARINATING: **4 hours**

INGREDIENTS

Serves 6

- 2 lb (900 g) swordfish fillet
- 2 large shallots
- 2 garlic cloves
- 2 long mild green chilis
- 2 limes
- ⅔ cup (150 ml) olive oil
- 1 tbsp brown sugar
- 2 cups (400 g) basmati rice
- 5½ oz (150 g) cashew nuts
- 1 heaped tbsp turmeric
- salt, freshly ground pepper

>> Peel and chop the shallots and garlic cloves. Wash and seed the chilis, and slice thinly. Wash the limes and reserve the zest; reserve the juice.

>> In a large bowl, mix the lime juice with salt and pepper. Add 7 tablespoons (100 ml) of olive oil, the chopped shallots and garlic, the sliced chilis, the lime zest, and the brown sugar. Beat the marinade together rapidly.

>> Cut the swordfish in approximately ⅝-inch (1.5-cm) cubes and thread on wooden skewers. Place the skewers in a deep dish and pour over the marinade. Cover with plastic film and refrigerate for 4 hours.

>> Cook the rice in a saucepan of boiling salted water following the instructions on the packet. Rinse under cold running water and leave to drain in a sieve.

>> Chop the cashew nuts coarsely.

>> In a dry skillet, toast the cashew nuts for 3 minutes over low heat. Add the turmeric and the remaining olive oil and brown for 2 minutes over medium heat. Add the cooked rice to the skillet and brown for 5 minutes, stirring with a spatula.

>> Drain the skewers, reserving the marinade, and cook under a broiler or in a dry skillet for 4–5 minutes on each side.

>> Serve with the rice and cashew nuts and a little of the marinade.

SKEWERS OF SALMON, BACON, AND PARMESAN WITH CHOPPED TOMATOES

PREPARATION: **40 minutes**
COOKING TIME: **15 minutes**

INGREDIENTS

Serves 6

- 2 lb (900 g) salmon fillets (without skin and bones)
- 3½ oz (100 g) Parmesan
- 18 thin strips bacon
- 10 medium tomatoes
- 4 large shallots
- 1 bunch fresh sage
- ⅔ cup (150 ml) olive oil
- salt, freshly ground pepper

» Cut the salmon in 18 equally sized cubes. Shave the Parmesan with a vegetable peeler.

» On the worktop, spread out the bacon strips and cover with Parmesan shavings. Place 1 cube of salmon on each strip; season with salt and pepper. Roll the bacon fairly tightly round the salmon.

» Thread 3 cubes of salmon and bacon on each wooden skewer and refrigerate.

» Wash the tomatoes and plunge in a saucepan of boiling water for 20 seconds. Drain and rinse under cold running water. Peel, cut in two, and remove the seeds. Chop the flesh with a knife.

» Peel and chop the shallots. Chop 6 sage leaves. In a large bowl, mix the chopped tomatoes with the chopped sage, shallots, 3½ tablespoons (50 ml) of olive oil, salt, and pepper, and refrigerate.

» Pick off the remaining sage leaves. Heat 3½ tablespoons (50 ml) of the oil in a pan and fry the sage leaves for 2 minutes over high heat. Drain on paper towels.

» Heat the remaining oil in a skillet or a broiler pan. Place the salmon skewers in it and cook for 5–6 minutes on each side over medium heat.

» Serve immediately with the cold chopped tomatoes and crispy sage leaves.

SKEWERS OF COD, BELL PEPPERS, AND CHORIZO WITH A MILD BELL PEPPER COULIS

PREPARATION: **40 minutes**
COOKING TIME: **1 hour**

INGREDIENTS

Serves 6

- 1¾ lb (800 g) cod loin
- 3 red bell peppers
- 2 yellow bell peppers
- ½ spicy chorizo
- 1 tsp red chili pepper
- 7 tbsp (100 ml) olive oil
- sea salt
- salt

» Pre-heat the oven to 355 °F (180 °C).

» Wrap the red bell peppers in a sheet of aluminum foil and place on a baking sheet. Bake in the oven for 45 minutes.

» Peel the yellow bell peppers with a vegetable peeler, de-seed, and cut in cubes.

» Remove the skin of the chorizo and cut in thin rounds.

» Cut the cod loin in small cubes.

» Thread the cubes of cod, yellow bell peppers, and rounds of chorizo alternately on wooden skewers. Place the skewers on a serving dish, sprinkle with red chili pepper and sea salt, and refrigerate.

» Remove the red bell peppers from the oven and leave to cool for 10 minutes in the foil. Then peel, de-seed under cold running water, and cut the flesh in pieces. Place them in a blender goblet with 3½ tablespoons (50 ml) of the olive oil, 7 tablespoons (100 ml) of cold water, and salt. Mix to a creamy coulis.

» Brush the skewers with the remaining olive oil. Heat a broiler pan, a large skillet, or a cooking plate and cook the skewers for 8–10 minutes over medium heat, turning regularly. Serve immediately with the bell pepper coulis, accompanied by a green salad or a salad of broiled bell peppers flavored with garlic.

SKEWERS OF ANGLERFISH AND BACON WITH PARSLEY AND GARLIC BUTTER

PREPARATION: **40 minutes**

COOKING TIME: **15 minutes**

INGREDIENTS

Serves 6

- 2¼ lb (1 kg) anglerfish fillets
- 1 bunch flat-leaf parsley
- 1 garlic clove
- 2 large shallots
- 10 tbsp (140 g) softened butter
- 1 tsp pastis
- 2 large bunches small scallions
- 18 thin strips smoked bacon
- 3½ tbsp (50 ml) olive oil
- 1 tbsp brown sugar
- salt, freshly ground pepper

≫ Wash and chop the parsley. Peel and chop the garlic and the shallots.

≫ In a large bowl, mix the butter with the garlic, shallots, parsley, pastis, and salt and pepper to taste, and refrigerate.

≫ Rinse the scallions, keeping a little of the green stem, and cut in two.

≫ Trim the anglerfish fillets (removing all the small pieces of skin and cartilage) and cut in 18 cubes. Season with salt and pepper. Wrap each cube fairly tightly in 1 strip of bacon. Thread 3 cubes of anglerfish in bacon on each wooden skewer.

≫ In a skillet, fry the scallions in half the olive oil for 2 minutes over high heat. Sprinkle with brown sugar and season with salt and pepper. Reduce the heat and cook for 4–6 minutes: they should be slightly caramelized but still crisp. Keep warm.

≫ Heat the remaining oil in a large skillet and cook the skewers over medium heat for 10 minutes, turning several times during cooking. Reduce the heat, add the parsley and garlic butter to the skillet, let it melt, and roll the skewers in it to coat them thoroughly.

≫ Serve the skewers with the scallions covered in parsley and garlic butter.

PREPARATION: **1 hour**
COOKING TIME: **20 minutes**

INGREDIENTS

Serves 6

- 3 large squid
- 8 thin slices of Parma ham
- 2 scallions
- 4 oz (120 g) pecorino
- 7 oz (200 g) mixed green and black olives
- 3½ tbsp (50 ml) olive oil + a little for serving
- salt, freshly ground pepper

Skewers of squid stuffed with olives, pecorino, and Parma ham

≫ Clean the squid under fresh running water, taking care not to pierce the tubes. Keep the heads and chop roughly.

≫ Chop the slices of ham. Peel and chop the scallions. Slice the tender green part of the stems and set aside for the end of the recipe. Grate the pecorino. Pit and chop the olives.

≫ In a skillet, sweat the chopped scallions in the olive oil for 3 minutes over medium heat. Add the squid heads and ham; season with salt and pepper. Cook for 6–8 minutes over medium heat, stirring continuously. Turn off the heat, add the olives and the grated pecorino. Mix together and leave to cool.

》 Cut each tube of squid in 4 identical pieces. Stuff these pieces with the mixture, packing it in well with a spoon. Thread the skewers by carefully inserting a wooden skewer through each side of the squid to keep the ends closed. Season with salt and pepper.

》 Heat a grill pan or a dry skillet and brown the skewers of squid lightly for 4—5 minutes on each side over high heat.

》 Sprinkle the skewers with slices of green scallion and drizzle with olive oil.

》 Serve with potato purée with olive oil.

SKEWERS OF SCALLOPS, POTATOES, AND ANDOUILLE SAUSAGE

PREPARATION: **45 minutes**
COOKING TIME: **30 minutes**

INGREDIENTS

Serves 6

- 18 medium scallops without coral
- 1¾ lb (750 g) large potatoes
- 2 cups (500 ml) cider
- 6 tbsp (80 g) granulated sugar
- 3 tbsp cider vinegar
- 2½ tbsp (40 g) butter
- 6 slices of andouille de Vire sausage about ¼ inch (4 mm) thick
- 3 tbsp olive oil
- salt, freshly ground pepper

> Peel and wash the potatoes. Cut rounds ¾ inch (2 cm) thick and, with a small cutter, cut "plugs" out of the rounds (keep the trimmings for potato purée). Boil these plugs of potato for 15 minutes in a saucepan of salted water (starting with the water cold).

> Meanwhile, in a saucepan, heat the cider with the sugar and vinegar for 10 minutes over medium heat to give a slightly golden caramel. Remove from the heat and mix in 1½ tablespoons (20 g) of the butter using a spatula. Transfer the caramel to a bowl and leave to cool.

> With the same cutter as for the potatoes, cut 18 rounds from the slices of sausage.

> Drain the potato plugs and rinse under cold running water. In a skillet, heat half the olive oil with 2 teaspoons (10 g) of the butter and brown the potatoes lightly for 3 minutes on each side over high heat. Transfer to a plate.

> On each of 18 wooden skewers, thread potato plugs, 1 scallop, and 1 round of sausage. Brown the skewers lightly in the skillet in the remaining butter and oil for 4–5 minutes over medium heat, turning several times during cooking. Season with salt and pepper.

> Serve the skewers, as an appetizer or a main course, with the warm cider caramel.

SKEWERS OF SHRIMP IN A THAI MARINADE, WITH RICE AND FRIED GINGER

PREPARATION: 30 minutes
MARINATING: 4 hours
COOKING TIME: 15 minutes

INGREDIENTS

Serves 6

- 42 medium shrimp
- 3½ oz (100g) fresh ginger
- 3 garlic cloves
- 10 leaves Thai basil or cilantro
- 1 small red chili
- 7 tbsp (100 ml) olive oil
- 1 cup (200 g) basmati rice
- 1 tsp squid ink (some supermarkets or ethnic stores)
- salt, freshly ground pepper
- oil for deep frying

» Carefully peel the shrimp, leaving the heads and tails on. Thread two skewers through each shrimp to keep them nice and straight. Place in a deep, wide dish.

» Peel the ginger and chop one-third of it. Peel and chop the garlic cloves. Wash and chop the basil (or cilantro). Wash, de-seed, and chop the chili.

» In a bowl, mix the olive oil with the chopped ginger, garlic, basil, chili, salt, and pepper. Pour this marinade over the skewers of shrimp. Cover the dish with plastic film and refrigerate for at least 4 hours.

» Cook the rice in a saucepan of boiling salted water, following the instructions on the packet. Rinse under cold running water and leave to drain in a sieve to leave it as dry as possible. Then mix the rice with the squid ink, spread on a baking sheet, and refrigerate.

» Cut the remaining part of the ginger in thin sticks.

» Heat the frying oil to 355 °F (180 °C) and fry the rice in small batches for 4–5 minutes and the ginger sticks for 3 minutes. Drain both on paper towels.

» Remove the excess marinade from the shrimp skewers. Heat a broiler pan or a large dry skillet and cook the shrimp for 4–5 minutes on each side over medium heat.

» Serve immediately with the crispy rice and fried ginger.

SKEWERS OF SUMMER VEGETABLES WITH ARUGULA PESTO

PREPARATION: 30 minutes
REFRIGERATION: 1 hour
COOKING TIME: 20 minutes

INGREDIENTS

Serves 6

- 2 small zucchini
- 2 yellow bell peppers
- 2 red bell peppers
- 1 small eggplant
- 6 large cherry tomatoes
- 1 large bunch scallions
- 2 tbsp oregano sprigs, dried or fresh
- sea salt
- ⅔ cup (150 ml) olive oil
- 5½ oz (150 g) arugula
- ½ cup (60 g) pine nuts
- 2 garlic cloves
- 2½ oz (75 g) grated Parmesan
- freshly ground pepper

> Wash all the vegetables. Cut the zucchini in rounds. Cut the eggplant in half lengthways and then in half-rounds. Cut the scallions in two. Peel and de-seed the bell peppers, then cut in pieces the same size as the zucchini rounds.

> Thread all the vegetables in turn on wooden skewers. Place the skewers on a serving dish and sprinkle with oregano and sea salt. Season with pepper and brush with olive oil. Refrigerate for 1 hour.

> Wash the arugula and plunge in a saucepan of boiling salted water for 20 seconds. Drain and rinse immediately in a bowl of very cold water. Squeeze out with your hands to extract as much water as possible. Chop roughly.

> Toast the pine nuts lightly in a dry skillet for 3 minutes over low heat. Leave to cool, then chop.

> Peel and chop the garlic. Transfer to a deep bowl. Add the arugula, the remaining olive oil, salt, and pepper. Mix for 2 minutes with a hand mixer. Add the Parmesan and pine nuts. Mix together well to give a smooth, even pesto.

> Heat a broiler pan, or a dry skillet, over medium heat and cook the vegetable skewers for 15–20 minutes, turning regularly.

> Serve immediately with the arugula pesto.

Serve the skewers on their own or to accompany red or white meat, or fish.

Skewers of cherry tomatoes in bacon with balsamic sauce

PREPARATION: **15 minutes**

COOKING TIME: **25 minutes**

INGREDIENTS

Serves 6

- 36 large cherry tomatoes
- 36 thin strips smoked bacon
- 3½ tbsp (50 ml) balsamic vinegar
- 1 tbsp granulated sugar
- 1 tbsp butter
- 3½ tbsp (50 ml) olive oil
- salt, freshly ground pepper

> Pre-heat the oven to 390 °F (200 °C).

> Pour the balsamic vinegar into a saucepan. Add the sugar, salt, and pepper. Bring to a boil, then reduce for 15 minutes over medium heat until the vinegar has a syrupy consistency. Remove from the heat and mix in the butter. Keep warm (but do not boil).

> Wash the cherry tomatoes and place them in a large bowl. Add the olive oil, salt, and pepper. Mix gently to cover the tomatoes with oil.

> Wrap each tomato tightly in 1 slice of bacon. Thread 3 tomatoes on each wooden skewer. Place the skewers on a baking sheet lined with parchment. Bake in the oven for 10 minutes.

> Arrange the skewers on plates and drizzle with balsamic sauce.

> Serve with small romaine lettuce hearts.

You can mix a little chopped oregano, basil, or sage with the tomatoes before wrapping them in the bacon.

SKEWERS OF PINEAPPLE WITH ALMOND CRUMBLE

PREPARATION: **30 minutes**
COOKING TIME: **25 minutes**

INGREDIENTS

Serves 6

- 1 large ripe pineapple
- 4 tbsp (55 g) butter
- 6½ tbsp (90 g) granulated sugar
- 1 level tsp ground cardamom
- 3½ tbsp (50 ml) brown rum

For the almond crumble
- ⅓ cup (75 g) softened butter
- 3½ tbsp (50 g) granulated sugar
- ⅔ cup (100 g) flour
- 3 oz (80 g) slivered almonds

> Pre-heat the oven to 355 °F (180 °C).

> Make the crumble first: in a bowl, mix the butter with the sugar. Add the flour and the split almonds, slightly crushed, and mix with your fingertips to give a crumbly dough. Spread this on a baking sheet lined with parchment and bake in the oven for 15—20 minutes. Remove the crumble from the oven and leave to cool on the baking sheet.

> Remove the skin, eyes, and core of the pineapple and cut the flesh in small cubes. Thread these on 12 small wooden skewers.

> In a large skillet, melt the butter and fry the skewers lightly for 2—3 minutes over medium heat. Dust with sugar, covering them well, then caramelize for 3—4 minutes over medium heat. Remove the skewers from the skillet.

> De-glaze the caramel from the skillet with 7 tablespoons (100 ml) of water over high heat. Add the rum and the ground cardamom, then reduce over high heat. Return the skewers to the sauce in the skillet to warm them up a little.

> Arrange the skewers on plates, sprinkle with crumble, and cover with sauce. Eat immediately.

You can replace the pineapple with mango: in that case, cook the skewers for only 2 minutes in the skillet.

SKEWERS OF FIGS WITH HONEY AND BANYULS

PREPARATION: 15 minutes
COOKING TIME: 10 minutes

INGREDIENTS

Serves 6

- 18 figs, not too ripe
- 3½ oz (100 g) whole almonds with skins
- ⅓ cup (80 g) butter
- 3½ oz (100 g) liquid honey
- generous ¾ cup (200 ml) banyuls
- 1 pinch pepper

> Wash the figs, remove the tops, and cut in half. Thread 3 fig halves on each wooden skewer.

> Chop the almonds coarsely with a knife.

> Melt 4 tbsp (50 g) butter in a large skillet. When the butter begins to sizzle, add the skewers, flesh side down, and cook for 3 minutes over high heat. Turn the skewers over and cook for 2 minutes. Transfer to a plate.

> Add the honey to the skillet and caramelize for 3 minutes over high heat. Then add the banyuls and reduce for 3–4 minutes over high heat. Beat in the pepper and the remaining butter, still over high heat.

> When the sauce is syrupy, add the almonds to the skillet, then carefully add the skewers. Warm them up for 3 minutes, spooning the sauce over them. Serve immediately.

Serve the fig skewers with a scoop of ice cream, accompanied by homemade French cookies such as financiers or madeleines.

MEASUREMENTS

LIQUID MEASURES

Metric System	American system	Other name
5 ml	1 teaspoon (French coffee spoon)	
15 ml	1 tablespoon (French soup spoon)	
35 ml	⅛ cup (French cup)	1 oz (or ounce)
65 ml	¼ cup or ¼ large glass	2 oz
125 ml	½ cup or ½ large glass	4 oz
250 ml	1 cup or 1 large glass	8 oz
500 ml	2 cups or 1 pint	
1 liter	4 cups or 2 pints	

WEIGHTS

Metric System	American system	Other name
30 g	1 oz	
55 g	⅛ lb	2 oz
115 g	¼ lb	4 oz
170 g	⅜ lb	6 oz
225 g	½ lb	8 oz
454 g	1 lb	16 oz

OVEN TEMPERATURES

Heat	° Celsius	Thermostat	° Fahrenheit
Very low	70 °C	Th. 2–3	150 °F
Low	100 °C	Th. 3–4	200 °F
	120 °C	Th. 4	250 °F
Medium	150 °C	Th. 5	300 °F
	180 °C	Th. 6	350 °F
Hot	200 °C	Th. 6–7	400 °F
	230 °C	Th. 7–8	450 °F
Very hot	260 °C	Th. 8–9	500 °F

Thanks to Aurélie, Anne, Pierre-Louis, and all the Mango team, who are always full of beans where the continuity of the Gueuletons collection is concerned.

Disclaimer
It is advisable not to serve dishes that contain raw eggs to very young children, pregnant women, elderly people, or to anyone weakened by serious illness. If in any doubt, consult your doctor. Be sure that all the eggs you use are as fresh as possible.

© Mango, Paris — 2015
Original title: *Boulettes ! Et brochettes à partager*
ISBN 978-23-17006-60-9

Editorial director: Anne la Fay
Editor: Aurélie Cazenave
Design management: Laurent Quellet et Armelle Riva
Layout: Natacha Marmouget
Proofreading and corrections: Armelle Heron
Production: Thierry Dubus, Marie Guibert

© for this English edition: h.f.ullmann publishing GmbH

Translation from French: Rae Walter in association with First Edition Translations Ltd, Cambridge, UK

Overall responsibility for production: h.f.ullmann publishing GmbH, Potsdam, Germany

Printed in India, 2016

ISBN 978-3-8480-1014-1

10 9 8 7 6 5 4 3 2 1
X IX VIII VII VI V IV III II I

www.ullmannmedien.com
info@ullmannmedien.com
facebook.com/hfullmann
twitter.com/hfullmann_int

MEATBALLS

In this series

FISH & MORE
[FISH AND SEAFOOD TO GRILL OR COOK]

MEATBALLS

MEATBA

CAKES
[FABULOUS RECIPES TO BAKE AND ENJOY]

MEATBALLS

MEATBALLS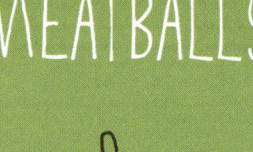

MEATBA

MEAT
[THE ART OF COOKING MEAT]

MEATBALLS

MEATBALLS

MEATBA

BURGERS
[BAGELS AND HOT DOGS]

MEATBALLS

MEATBALLS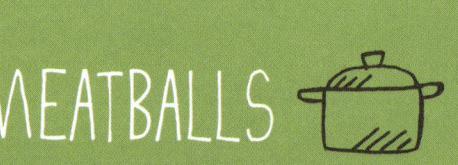

PASTA
[FRESH, SIMPLE, AND DELICIOUS]

MEATBALLS

MEATBALLS

MEATBA

MEATBALLS